EASY-TO-MAKE
OUTDOOR PLAY EQUIPMENT

THE MACMILLAN COMPANY
NEW YORK · CHICAGO
DALLAS · ATLANTA · SAN FRANCISCO
LONDON · MANILA

BRETT-MACMILLAN LTD.
TORONTO

Easy-To-Make Outdoor Play Equipment

by
Reginald R. Hawkins

THE MACMILLAN COMPANY

New York—1957

Library of Congress catalog card number: 57–5773

PREFACE

This book provides directions and suggestions for the construction of about 40 different kinds of play equipment for children. Included are most of the standard devices and, in addition, some unusual and novel ones. Every one is suitable for use outdoors, and a fair number of the devices can be enjoyed indoors as well. The lawn swing for small children, for example, is as much fun on a rainy day in a basement playroom as it is outdoors on a sunny day.

All of the equipment can be constructed with simple hand tools and with no more than a meager knowledge of how to use them. In fact, such an article as the Baby's Swing is an excellent project for gaining experience in woodworking. Although the book is addressed primarily to parents, older children, particularly boys who are taking manual training in high school, will find things in it that they can make. The chinning bar that hangs on the side of a building is something that a high-school student might make in the school shop, then use to develop his athletic prowess.

The book is more than a mere collection of projects. It is my hope that it will inspire in many, many families a cooperative program of play-equipment construction that will be fun for both parents and children.

REGINALD R. HAWKINS

CONTENTS

EASY-TO-MAKE
OUTDOOR PLAY EQUIPMENT

INTRODUCTION

A certain amount of creativeness must be put into the construction of successful playthings of the kinds described in this book. Readers will find that in numerous instances I have not given precise dimensions. The reason is that a plaything such as a swing or climbing apparatus should be designed for the family of children who will use it whether this family consists of one child or seven. Children vary greatly in strength, coordination, and venturesomeness. Some children 6 years of age are interested only in toys that test their daring, while others of the same age are still playing happily in sandboxes. A strong, athletic boy or girl will be ready for a device such as the horizontal ladder two or three years before another boy who likes gentle, unaggressive play.

DESIGNING

No one is in a better position than parents to judge the kind of play equipment their children would use. In addition, parents are best situated to measure their children and on the basis of these measurements to design play equipment intelligently. How high should the swing be from the ground for a certain child? The only answer of any value to that question is one based on measuring the child and observing his physical capabilities. The problem of designing for several children is more complex, but again the approach to it is the same. This approach might be summed up as: observe, measure, and think.

SAFETY

The problem of safety is a difficult one. Children will occasionally fall, but keeping high equipment away from children will not do any good because it is important to them to learn to avoid falling. The best that a parent can do is to keep such equipment off hard surfaces. Play equipment should be strongly made, and important parts that wear or deteriorate in strength, such as swing ropes, should be inspected from time to time. In designing and building a toy that has moving parts, the parent can avoid joints and small gaps in which children's fingers might be severely pinched.

WOOD

Selection of wood for outdoor play equipment is simple in comparison to its selection for such crafts as cabinetmaking. The species used in your locality for house framing will usually prove to be the best choices for lumber for the devices in this book.

Woods are divided in the trade into softwoods and hardwoods. The first group includes such well known ones as Southern pine, Douglas fir, and California redwood. Included in the hardwoods are white oak, red oak, hard maple, and beech. Most of the hardwoods are harder than the common softwoods. They are somewhat more difficult to work with hand tools, but they do not form splinters readily and, in most instances, hold screws somewhat better. Their main use in outdoor toys is for such parts as seats and ladder rungs. The softwoods are easier to work. Most of them will form splinters if rubbed hard against the grain, but splinter formation can be controlled to a considerable extent by rounding sharp corners and by protecting the wood with paint or varnish.

Resistance to decay and to subterranean termites are two qualities very desirable in the parts of play equipment that are buried in the ground or that rest on the ground. Only two native woods, California redwood and Southern cypress, are given credit for substantial natural resistance to both these enemies. Most other woods require treatment with a wood preservative if they are to last more than two years in the soil. A widely used wood preservative is the chemical pentachlorophenol. Solutions of this chemical are available in hardware stores and building-supply houses under various trade names. Do not depend upon brushing this material on the wood; instead, arrange to soak the wood in it.

I have found that a handy method of application is to use a discarded vegetable bin from a refrigerator. I put this large pan on the floor in the corner of my garage. Then I stand the wood in the over-sized pan and lean it against the garage wall. I pour in the wood preservative to the top of the pan, then let the wood stand in it from 24 hours to a week, depending upon the thickness of the pieces. It is usually necessary to add a little more preservative to the pan during a long period of soaking.

Because pentachlorophenol is somewhat toxic, follow the manufacturer's directions carefully and keep children away from the pan. In addition, the solvents are usually flammable, and must not be handled near fire.

Rounding of corners to control splinters is done by planing or sanding off the sharp corners of the lumber so as to form a rounded rather than a square edge. Because painting or varnishing tends to hold the surface of any wood, it is a means of retarding the development of splinters. On play equipment that will be used by small children it is essential to avoid toxic paints. Primarily this means to avoid paints containing lead compounds. Before using paint on a plaything for a small child, read the label to see if there is any lead in the pigment. There are now many exterior house paints on the market that contain no poisonous materials.

Sometimes a clear finish rather than an opaque paint is desired. In selecting such a finish, be certain that the manufacturer specifies it for outdoor use. For finishing redwood, there are specially formulated finishes that tend to preserve the original appearance of the wood. Unless these are used, the attractive reddish brown of the fresh wood will change under outdoor exposure to an uninteresting grayish brown. Shingle stains are useful when the main object is to stain wood in a desired color.

Plywood is a very useful material in constructing outdoor play equipment. It is sold in standard-size panels. Some dealers have panels as small as 4 ft. by 4 ft., but often the only size stocked is 4 ft. by 8 ft. Occasionally a dealer will have 4-ft. panels in longer lengths. Only exterior-type plywood is suitable for structures that will be exposed to the weather. This type is made with an adhesive which is not affected by water. However, rain will cause the outer plies to wrinkle slightly and become rough unless the wood is protected. Therefore, paint or varnish exterior-type plywood if you wish it to remain smooth. Exterior-type plywood is also manufactured with plastic surfaces. I have not used these in toymaking, but suggest that you may wish to investigate them. The plastic surface does not become rough and does not require painting.

ROPE

Braided cotton clothesline is not a safe material from which to hang a swing, although one sometimes finds it being used for that purpose. For swings and other play equipment where rope supports considerable weight, use only manila rope of the best available grade. Hardware stores and general mail-order stores supply it in all the common sizes.

References are made later in the book to a "whipped" joint in rope. Whipping in this sense is a method of securing a joint so that it will not become loose. The technique is illustrated in Fig. 1 .There is no space in this book for a description of knots and rope splicing, although some elementary knowledge of knots and of rope splicing is useful in making outdoor play equipment. Public libraries usually have several books on knots and splices that cover this field.

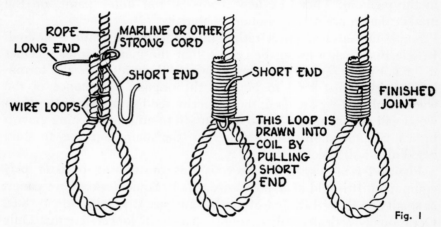

ROPE — LONG END
MARLINE OR OTHER STRONG CORD
SHORT END
WIRE LOOPS
SHORT END
THIS LOOP IS DRAWN INTO COIL BY PULLING SHORT END
FINISHED JOINT

Fig. 1

CONCRETE

Standard concrete is made of Portland cement, sand, and gravel. These ingredients are combined in various proportions which are indicated by numerals arranged thus: 1:3:5. This formula indicates parts by volume in this order: Portland cement, sand, gravel; thus 1 part Portland cement; 3 parts sand; 5 parts gravel. Incidentally 1:3:5 is a standard mix, good for such uses as foundations, placing around posts, etc.

The simplest way to mix concrete is to buy it mixed. It can be purchased dry in paper sacks with the ingredients already mixed.

4

Only water needs to be added to this proprietary product. It can also be purchased wet from suppliers of ready-mixed concrete, but a small quantity cannot be bought in this way—only quantities such as would be required for the making of a long walk, or the artificial brook described in this book.

The ingredients of concrete can be mixed by hand on a smooth, firm surface such as a wooden platform. The gravel is put down first, the sand on top of it, and the cement shaken over the sand. The whole pile is turned with a shovel until it looks uniformly gray. Then a hole is formed in the middle of the pile and the water poured in. The pile is then turned carefully so as to mix the dry materials into the water without spilling the latter. It is important not to put in too much water. A moderately stiff mix that can be shoveled makes stronger concrete than one that runs like water. Stiff concrete should be "worked" a little with a spade or shovel as it is placed in order to avoid pockets filled only with air. The surface is produced by "floating," that is, rubbing the surface while the concrete is still wet. Rubbing with a wooden float, or block of wood, will produce a grainy surface; with a steel trowel, a smooth, slick surface.

Once in place, concrete must not be allowed to dry out before it cures. Cover exposed surfaces with some absorbent material such as leaves or hay and keep it damp for 24 to 48 hours.

LEVELING AND PLUMBING

Most outdoor play equipment must be placed so that it is level and plumb in order to function satisfactorily. This applies even to the factory-made steel swings, although many are put up in yards without attention to such matters. Levelness is easily determined by use of a carpenter's or mason's level with its familiar bubbles in small glass tubes. All but the cheapest levels have glasses positioned so as to test either levelness or plumbness.

To find out whether a structure is level, the instrument is placed on it horizontally; to find out whether it is plumb, it is held against it in a vertical position. When an irregular piece of wood is involved, such as a pole for a swing, plumbness can be tested more easily with a plumb bob. This simple instrument is simply held by its cord near the upright pole and more or less parallel to it, while someone stands off at a short distance and judges whether the true axis of the pole is parallel to the cord holding the bob.

5

FASTENERS

Practically every reader of this book will know that nails are available in various lengths (and diameters) designated by an antiquated "penny" system, thus 4-penny, 6-penny, etc.—the more "pennies," the longer the nail. Common nails have moderately thick shanks and flat heads; box nails have thinner shanks and flat heads; finishing nails have slender heads. Most nails sold are made of steel. Unfortunately, when used in outdoor play equipment, the steel heads soon rust and create ugly spots. The rust will even stain through outdoor paint sometimes. Aluminum nails are not subject to rusting. They cost a little more than steel nails, but their chief disadvantage is that not all hardware stores stock them.

Screws come in many varieties, but the one that is of most interest in making play equipment is the common wood screw with a flat head. Round-headed wood screws are used when it is desirable to put a washer under the head. Both varieties are manufactured in both brass and steel. Brass screws are good but costly. Fortunately, steel screws are available with zinc coatings that delay rusting though they do not prevent it. These screws are sold as "zinc-plated" or "galvanized"—the terms mean essentially the same.

The diameters of screws are designated by a number: No. 8, No. 10, etc. When buying screws, their lengths also must be stated, thus: No. 10 wood screws, 2 in. long. In selecting screws for length, it is necessary to pay attention to their function in the structure. For example, a screw that will serve only to hold one board against another need not penetrate as deeply as one that must support a considerable load. Screws used for such purposes as attaching swing hooks should penetrate 1½ in. or more into the wood that will bear the load. Wood screws of all but the smallest diameters require pre-drilled holes. A drill about ⅔ the diameter of the screw should be used to make the hole. Lag screws (Fig. 2 A) are heavy-duty fasteners. They come in various lengths and diameters, larger then common screws. They require pre-drilled holes. For a large lag screw, the diameter of the hole can be only slightly (10%–20%) less than the diameter of the screw.

Bolts of the type known as carriage bolts (Fig. 2 B) are the kind most often used in outdoor play equipment. These have a squared section under the head that engages the wood and prevents the bolt from turning. Carriage bolts are good fasteners for wooden parts not subject to twisting or turning forces. Machine bolts which have square

6

heads designed to be held or turned with a wrench should be used to fasten parts that tend to twist or turn. Flat washers (Fig. 2 D) or lock washers (Fig. 2 E) may be used under the nuts on carriage bolts and under both the heads and nuts of machine bolts. Eyebolts (Fig. 2 C and F) are useful in such applications as hanging of swings. The variety without a gap in the metal (Fig. 2 F) is stronger and costs more.

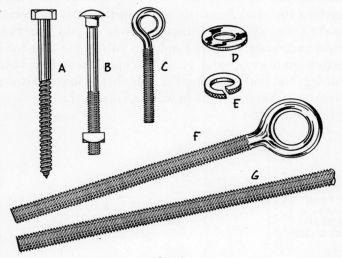

Fig. 2

Hardware stores usually do not stock carriage and machine bolts in lengths greater than 6 in. or 8 inches. However, many do have threaded rods (Fig. 2 G) in 3-ft. lengths. These may be cut to the desired length and fitted with nuts. Bolts and tie rods longer than 3 ft. must usually be made by threading the ends of steel rods. Such work is done by blacksmith shops and machine shops.

Most standard bolts are available in a zinc-plated finish. Rusting of bolts and nuts with black finish can be controlled by painting (after they are in place) with a non-toxic metal paint.

Sandbox with Canopy *(fig. 3)*

This is the common, back-yard variety of sandbox for children of pre-school ages. Similar ones are sold by the hundreds of thousands every year. The cheapest of the factory-made ones often do not last out one summer. The best are not superior to the homemade one pictured here provided it is made of suitable materials.

Because this box stands up on stout legs, earthworms cannot work their way into the sand from the soil beneath. It is large enough to accommodate two children without crowding, and the two board seats provide adequate space not only for sitting but also for holding a satisfactory number of sand pies and cupcakes. A few ¼-in. holes bored through the bottom along the side that is lowest after the box is placed where it will be played in will provide all the drainage needed to get rid of rain water.

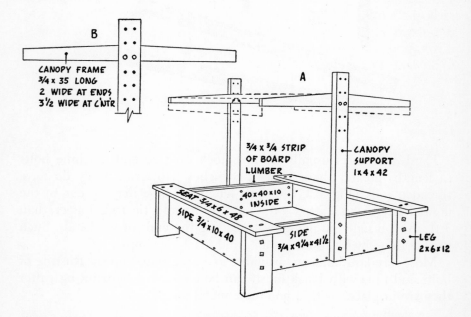

The commercial boxes usually have slotted canopy supports and a single bolt at each side of the canopy frame that must be loosened in order to adjust the canopy. This construction invites children to attempt to adjust the canopy themselves, with the result that sometimes another child playing in the sand gets bumped on the head. Because a sandbox canopy does not require frequent adjustment, a safe method is better than a convenient one. The pairs of holes and carriage bolts (Fig. 3 A and B) shown provide an adjustment that is easy for an adult but too complicated to be attempted by a child.

The usual way of making the canopy is to construct a framework of slats and to cover this with awning material. Awning material deteriorates, as most householders know. A more durable canopy can be made by using exterior-type plywood of ¼-in. thickness. This plywood should be painted, and, of course, it may be painted in stripes if you prefer an awning effect. The hanging side pieces corresponding to the fringed ends of the traditional awning are made of separate strips of the same plywood material and are finished similarly.

The box itself may be made of tongued-and-grooved board lumber or exterior-type plywood. The latter is preferred, but if it is used the two edges not protected by the seats should be finished with a strip of board lumber as shown in order to prevent fraying of the edges of the plywood. If a softwood is used for the seats, canopy uprights, etc., it is important to round the corners and edges and to paint it in order to prevent the development of splinters.

Recommended Materials

Lumber

Box sides and bottom: ¾-in. exterior-type plywood, or ¾-in. tongued-and-grooved pine or other inexpensive, durable softwood.

Seats and canopy uprights: Oak or other splinter-resistant wood preferred. Pine, fir, and other softwoods may be used if necessary.

Canopy frame: Pine or other suitable softwood for the ends; ¼-in. exterior-type plywood for the cover.

Legs: Pine or other suitable softwood; or redwood, or cypress if decay resistance is desired.

Hardware

For fastening the box sides and bottom: No. 6 1½-in. brass screws (expensive), or zinc-plated steel screws, same size, or 5-penny aluminum nails. Nails may be spaced about 1½ in. apart; screws, 2½ in. apart. Pre-drill holes for screws, but not for nails.

For securing the legs and canopy uprights to the box and the canopy frame to the uprights: ¼-in. zinc-plated carriage bolts. Four of them should have wing nuts.

For attaching plywood to the canopy frame: 3-penny aluminum common nails.

Inexpensive, Expendable Sandbox *(fig. 4)*

This kind of sandbox is fairly satisfactory if you have a moderately dry place such as a patio floor on which to put it down for the season. It has no bottom and, therefore, is not to be recommended for placing on a grassy lawn or wet soil. The best way to manage such a box is to put it where it is to stay, fill it about two-thirds full of sand, and turn the children into it. If and when it becomes necessary to move it, an adult can lift the box away from the sand; then the sand can be shoveled up.

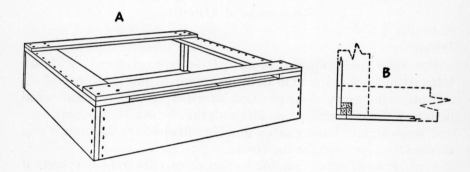

Almost any board lumber is suitable for this box. Lumber of 1-in. nominal thickness makes a stronger box, but the nominal ¾-in. thickness is more convenient to purchase and to work. The box can be built without the 2-in. by 2-in. posts in the interiors of the corners (Fig. 4 B). However, they make it stronger. Wherever nail points break through to the inside of the box, they should be clinched, that is, turned over.

Recommended Materials

Lumber

Box sides: No. 2 pine or almost any other construction lumber offered commercially. Redwood is excellent.

Seat boards: Oak or other splinter-resistant hardwood, or No. 1 pine or other suitable softwood.

Interior posts: No. 2 pine or other softwood with good nail- and screw-holding properties.

Hardware

For fastening the box sides: 6-penny common nails or, if you wish to avoid rust stains, aluminum nails of the same size.

For fastening the corners: No. 10 1½-in. zinc-plated wood screws or, if the box is built for only one season's use, 8-penny common nails.

Sandbox Supercolossal *(fig. 5)*

Sand play is not necessarily limited to children of pre-school age. At almost any beach in the summer one can see older children and even adults making things of sand. The character of sand play changes. Very young children are fascinated with making such things as pies and cakes and pouring sand from one vessel to another. Older children tend to construct models of landscape features such as roadways and tunnels, even mountain ranges. In the author's own yard is a sandbox, similar to the one pictured, which measures 12 ft. by 16 ft. and which is often used by more than half-a-dozen children at one time, usually working on a cooperative project of their own devising.

Obviously sandbox is not an appropriate name for this structure, but it is used because of the lack of another. In my own there is a stone wall at one end, while the other end is open just as shown (Fig. 5 A). However, a cabinet is better than a stone wall because it provides space for the storage of a variety of shovels, pans, and toys.

Washed sand of the quality used in making concrete is purchased a truckload at a time and placed inside the structure. The sand rests directly on the soil, which is not topsoil but a semi-clay subsoil free of organic matter.

In the course of play, children do throw sand over the sides. The pile gradually flattens and tends to flow out at the open end of the structure. Returning it, or a considerable fraction of it, is made simple by a board pavement on the outside. Once a week or so, the spilled sand is simply swept up and thrown back. A stone or brick pavement would catch the sand as well.

Obviously the dimensions of a box of this kind depend, first, on the space available for it and, second, on the number of children who will make use of it. The author's own box is probably as large as any family will have need for. As stated, it measures 12 ft. by 16 ft. If only two children will make use of the box, 8 ft. by 10 ft. would probably be an adequate area.

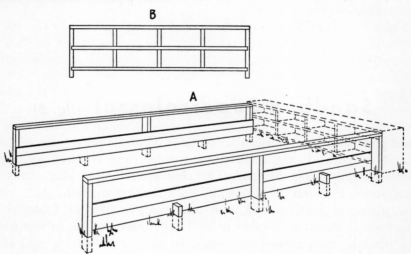

The main posts, top rails, and the short posts that come midway between the main posts may all be made either of 4 by 4's or 2 by 6's, that is to say, lumber 4 in. by 4 in. or 2 in. by 6 in. in cross section. In my opinion, 4 by 4's make a more attractive structure. Boards of ¾-in. thickness are adequate for the sides provided they are braced between the main posts. Two boards 8 in. wide make a total height of 16 in., which is, in my experience, enough. However, some home-owners may wish to run the boards all the way up the sides. Solid boarding makes the structure look more like a box, and therefore less pleasing in a yard. On the other hand, it does retain the sand better.

Because the top rail will be used for a walk, if the children who are to use the structure are rather young its height should not be more than 2½ feet. Children of 8 years and up get more fun out of striding on a taller structure, but perhaps they should have a fence similar to those described later in this book.

The cabinet at the end is a convenience rather than a necessity. If you choose not to make a cabinet, the end can be closed with boards, braced as along the sides. The dimensions of the cabinet, except for its depth, are determined by the rest of the structure. A depth of 1 ft. is adequate for most sand toys. It is a good idea to provide at least one compartment for each child who will make regular use of the sandbox. If the cabinet is made as shown in the sketch (Fig. 5 B), the lower compartments will tend to fill with sand and therefore should not be counted on for storage.

There are three good ways of attaching the top rails to the main posts. They may be doweled and glued; nails or screws may be driven through the rails into the posts; or angle irons and screws may be used to attach the underside of the rails to the posts. I prefer the last method. Galvanized angle irons or corner braces can be purchased in every store that sells hardware. A pair placed side by side under the rail is used at the joints between the rails and the end posts. A single brace is used under the rail on each side of intermediate posts.

Recommended Materials

Lumber

Posts: Redwood or cypress. If other wood is used, treat it with a wood preservative.

Side boards and top rails: Redwood preferred. No. 2 pine, or other softwood, may be used. Treatment with wood preservative should not be necessary because of the ease with which these parts can be replaced.

Hardware

For securing the top rails to the posts: ⅝ in. by 2½ in. by 2½ in. galvanized inside corner braces, and No. 9 zinc-plated wood screws 1¼ in. long.

For fastening the side boards and cabinet: Aluminum nails, or zinc-plated screws.

Standard Swing *(fig. 6)*

Not many years ago when the children of a family desired a swing, father or grandfather looked for a strong, horizontal limb on a tree not too far from the house. Some very exhilarating swings were made in this way, for the branch chosen was usually many feet off the ground and the swing ropes were long. In recent years factory-made swings on steel frames have made swings available to many children whose families do not happen to possess trees with suitable limbs. They have also removed the incentive for some fathers or grandfathers to put up a swing even when a good limb is available.

The ropes are never very long on factory-made swings; hence the excitement of a high swing is unknown to many of today's children. Furthermore, the factory-made swings have tended to limit the fun of swinging to rather small children, whereas in the old days children of all the school ages and even adults enjoyed swinging.

A swing such as the one sketched in Fig. 6 will not be needed if you have a tree with a stout branch in the right place, provided, of course, that the tree stands where it is practical to put up a swing. When a tree limb is lacking, this swing is a fair substitute. The heights noted on the drawing make a swing suitable for children from about 6 years to about 12 years of age. If the swing is to be used primarily by teen-aged children and young adults, the posts should be made taller. A height of 10 or 12 ft. is not too much for a swing designed for these ages.

The posts need be no more than 3 ft. apart for one swing, but a width between posts of 5 ft. is necessary for two swings, and 6 ft. is better. Whatever the width, the corner braces should connect with the top crosspiece at a point 3 or 4 in. short of where they would interfere with the swing ropes. These corner braces should be bolted as shown in Fig. 6 B. The lag screw which passes through the crosspiece into the post (also shown in B) should penetrate the upright post at least 2 inches.

A piece of lumber 4 in. by 6 in. in cross section is large enough for the crosspiece for a single swing with posts 3 ft. apart as shown in Fig. A; but if the frame is made for two swings and if the posts are spaced 5 ft. or 6 ft. apart, it is better to use a crosspiece 6 in. by 6 in. in cross section. Similarly, if a taller swing is made, lumber larger than 6 in. by 6 in. in cross section may be necessary for the posts. In fact, small

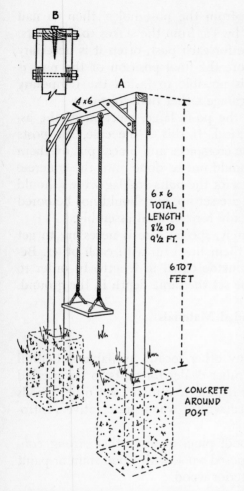

poles such as are used for rural utility lines make very good uprights for adult-size swings.

Because it is important to construct a swing of this kind so that strenuous "pumping" by two youngsters will not loosen the posts, concrete should be placed around the posts. A block of concrete 12 in. by 12 in. in cross section is big enough for a swing for youngsters, but the cross-sectional area should be increased to at least 18 in. by 18 in. if the swing will be used by near grownups. The recommended depth of the concrete depends, in regions with winters, on the depth to which the ground freezes in winter. The concrete should extend a few inches below the frost line. A minimum depth where the ground does not freeze is 2 ft. for the lower height; 2½ ft. for the taller.

It is a good idea to have a few inches of concrete under the posts, but this is difficult for amateur builders to manage. An alternative scheme is to place a flat stone or a chunk of concrete block in the bottom of the hole before the concrete is poured and to stand the post on it.

Erection of the swing frame requires advance planning. If a swing of about the height shown is being built, the frame should be put together on the ground. After the holes are dug, the frame is stood in them and made plumb (Introduction). It is necessary to hold the frame rigidly while the concrete is being poured and for about 24 hours afterward.

The usual method of holding is to drive stakes made of 2 by 4's

15

into the ground 6 or 8 ft. away from the post holes, then to nail temporary braces, also made of 2 by 4's, from the stakes to the posts. At least three braces are advisable for each post; often it is necessary to adjust them several times before the final position of the post is achieved. In some locations, it is possible to fasten the temporary braces to a nearby tree or to the garage rather than to stakes.

If the swing is a tall one and the posts large, erection of the assembled frame may not be practical. If this is the case, the posts must be erected separately and the crosspiece and braces put on them afterward from a ladder. (This should not be done until the concrete has cured for about a week.) Holes for the bolts and lag screws should be bored in the posts before they are set up, but should not be bored in the crosspiece until you are ready for the final assembly.

When the posts are set separately, special care is necessary to get each one plumb and also to get them lined up with each other. Before setting, the poles should be made equal in length. In order to get their tops even, they should be set the same depth in the ground.

Recommended Materials

Lumber

Upright posts: Redwood or any other locally available structural lumber recommended by your lumber dealer for posts to be inserted in the ground. Redwood will not require treatment, but other woods (except cypress) should be treated with a wood preservative (Introduction).

Crosspiece and braces: Redwood, pine, or any other strong construction lumber. Paint all the exposed wood with wood stain or paint designed for the protection of exterior wood.

Hardware

½-in.-diameter zinc-plated carriage bolts. ½-in.-diameter zinc-plated lag screws.

Swing hangers: Read the discussion of swing fittings accompanying Fig. 11.

Pump Swing *(fig. 7)*

The pump swing is a natural plaything for the 5- to 9-year group. It requires more effort to make it go than other kinds of swings, and therefore is an effective device for working off excess juvenile energy. Besides, it is lots of fun. It is not so well suited to outdoor installation as the other kinds of swings described in this book primarily because it requires three points of suspension overhead. A good place for it is a screened or open porch where it can be hung from the roof rafters or from lumber attached to them. Basements are good, too, because the suspending hooks can be attached firmly to the underside of the first floor joists of the house.

To operate this swing, the child sits on the seat facing forward and looking out between the pair of ropes. He places his feet on the stirrup piece below the seat and his hands on the bar to which the pair of ropes is attached. He pulls with his hands and simultaneously pushes with his feet, then pushes with his hands and relaxes his feet. The pulls and pushes soon set up a vigorous swinging action.

A swing can be built for one child or for two or three. Usually it is better to design it for two children even though there is only one child in the family because visiting playmates are certain to want a ride. A long seat board is necessary so that the child can bend his back without interference from the rear rope. For one child a seat board measuring 22 in. from front to back is long enough. Two children can sit on a seat of this length, but they will be more comfortable on one that is 26 to 30 in. long. Eight inches is an adequate width for the wide part of the seat, and 4 in. for the narrower part at the front. The narrowed portion should extend back from the front edge 10 to 12 in.

A good piece of dressed lumber of nominal 1-in. thickness free of splits and knots should be selected for the seat. The board should be planed and sanded smooth on its upper side and all edges rounded. If 1-in. pipe is used for the "front end," the cutout in the board to accommodate the pipe should be approximately 1½ in. by 3 in., the longer dimension being in the direction of the seat's length.

As shown at A, the "front end" of this swing is made of galvanized steel pipe and fittings. Pipe of 1-in. nominal diameter is recommended. The bottom portion is formed of a standard tee and two pieces of pipe 4 in. long. These short lengths of pipe are called "nip-

17

ples" in the plumbing trade. The upper end is formed of a tee and two 3-in. nipples. The length of the pipe that runs from top to bottom and connects with the center tees should be 3 or 4 ft. long, depending upon whether the swing is built for pre-school children or older ones. The attachment with the seat is made at the midpoint of the pipe; in other words, the long pipe is divided evenly above and below the seat.

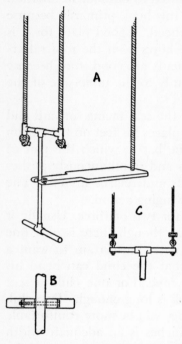

The attachment with the seat requires drilling through the pipe and using a machine bolt to form a pivot (Fig. 7 B). For really durable construction the hole through the pipe should be made large enough to accommodate a bronze bushing for the bolt. The bolt is, of course, passed through this bushing. Because making such a bushing requires some expert machine-shop work, most amateur toy-makers are satisfied with a simpler bearing consisting of a ¼-in. bolt passed through a hole which is slightly larger. If oiled lightly once in a while, this simple bearing will last a considerable length of time. Flat steel washers may be used on both sides of the pipe to hold it out of contact with the wood of the seat board.

The front ropes may be attached to the swing by passing them through the tees and knotting them well as illustrated in Fig. 7 A. Fig. 7 C shows an alternative method of joining them. As can be seen in this drawing, eyebolts (Fig. 2) are passed through holes drilled in the ends of the nipples. The rope ends are passed through the eyebolts and are fastened with rope clamps (Fig. 11 C). The rear rope is passed through a hole bored in the seat board and secured by a firm knot.

Hammock hooks, or porch swing hooks, purchasable at practically all hardware stores, are good things for attaching the ropes to the rafters or other framework overhead. These hooks should be sturdy and should be fastened securely. They should have the same spacing in relation to one another as the spacing of the ropes where these attach to the swing. Because of this requirement, it is sometimes advisable to change the dimensions of the seat a little to fit the best points of attachment overhead. If the ropes are spaced the same, top and bottom, the swing will fly straight; otherwise, it will tend to swing askew.

Recommended Materials

Lumber

See discussion above.

Hardware

Galvanized steel pipe and galvanized tees. Zinc-plated steel machine bolt (1 needed) 5/16-in. diameter, 4 in. long. (Optional) zinc-plated steel eyebolts ¼-in. diameter (2 needed). Rope clamps (2 needed) to fit diameter of rope used.

Baby's Swing *(fig. 8)*

Most babies enjoy swinging even before they are able to walk, but they cannot maintain their balance on a board swing. The swing sketched in Fig. 8 is for babies and babies only. It has sides and a front to prevent falling out. Part of it looks like familiar play blocks. Though there is plenty of room to squirm around in it, several minutes of struggling are required in order to stand up, if standing up can be managed at all.

Construction of a swing of this kind is an exercise in simple woodworking. All of the pieces are small. Fastening is easy, for it involves nailing only four pieces to the swing bottom. The swing ropes pass through all the others and serve to hold them together.

It would be a mistake to attempt to make this swing from anything but high-grade lumber. However, short ends left over from more ambitious projects may be used. A hardwood that is not too difficult to work is to be preferred. The holes that are bored to receive the ropes should be carefully placed in all the pieces; otherwise, misalignment will show up when the ropes are passed through. This swing is suitable for use both indoors and outdoors.

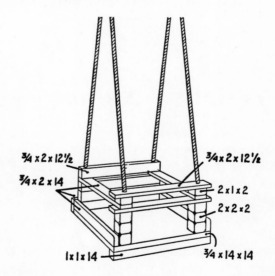

Ropes for a swing of this kind should not be more than 4 or 5 ft. long; hence, suspension is sometimes a problem. For outdoor use a wooden frame can be designed, or a tree limb at the right height can be found on some home sites. Indoors, a frame may be used, but unless carefully placed it will be in the way. In some houses it is possible to find a little-used doorway across which a bar or pole can be placed at an appropriate height for hanging the swing. Some of the poles and attachments used for hanging poles in closets can be converted to this use. Good quality manila rope as small as ½ in. in diameter is strong enough for a swing of this kind. The holes for the rope should be bored about ⅛ in. larger.

Probably the best finish for outdoor use is a clear lacquer or varnish formulated for outdoor finishing. If the swing is to be used indoors, colored paints are appropriate, and you may as well use your imagination in combining colors. Babies, as every parent soon learns, are fascinated by bright colors.

The four pieces that are attached directly to the seat board are nailed or screwed to it before the varnishing or painting is done. The pieces through which the ropes pass are finished before assembly. When all pieces are dry, the ropes are passed downward through the various pieces as shown in the drawing and emerge through the holes in the seat board. Here knots are tied in them, knots large enough so that there will be no danger of their being pulled back through the board.

A Variety of Swings *(fig. 9)*

Illustrated in Fig. 9 are a number of possible variations of the lower end of standard rope swings. At A is shown a narrow, rather firm board for high-flying experts. Not more than 4 in. in width and about 18 in. long, this board is suited both to sitting swinging and standing swinging. It should be made of a 1-in.-thick piece of oak or other strong lumber which is free of knots and other imperfections that might weaken it.

At B is shown a "log" swing. From a section of tree limb 3 to 4 in. in diameter, a straight piece 18 to 24 in. is cut. The bark is removed, and about 3 in. inward from each end a groove is whittled or turned. The purpose of the grooves is to hold the ropes in place. The ropes are attached by passing them around the log and knotting them firmly, as shown.

At *C* is shown a pair of steel rings. These are usually seen in gymnasiums, but they are just as attractive for exercise and acrobatics outdoors. These rings must be purchased, and they can be obtained from dealers in sporting goods. I know of no homemade substitute. The ropes are attached by knotting, or by whipped joints (Fig. 1); or a spliced joint may be employed.

At *D* is shown a knotted rope. This device, very challenging to boys of the 8 to 14 age group, can be hung at one end of a tall swing frame or suspended from the limb of a tree. Rope of fairly large diameter, ⅝ in. or more, should be used in order to get knots large enough for new climbers. The knots should be spaced 1 to 1½ ft. apart.

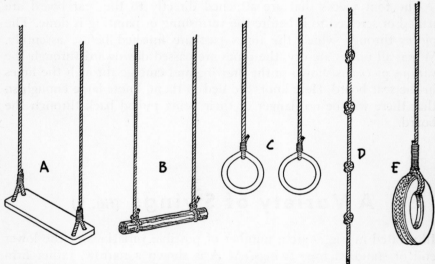

The swing shown at *E* was very popular in the days of the Model T Ford. Although not a rarity now, it is much less common, and the reason may be that it is more difficult to find discarded automobile tires with large enough holes in the center. The old 30 by 3½ clincher tires made good swings of this kind. Fortunately, such tires can still be found at automobile junk yards, and sometimes tire dealers will have some among their piles of used tires. Some present-day truck tires are also good. Except that it requires only a single rope, a tire swing has no special advantage over other kinds. Boys seem to like them, and a boy on a farm will often rig one himself.

Swing Boards *(fig. 10)*

There is variety even in the ways of attaching swing boards. Four popular methods are shown in Fig. 10. At A is sketched the simplest kind of fastening. Holes are simply bored through the board at four points near the ends, and the rope is passed through them. There are various ways of securing the rope after it is passed through, but the bound or whipped joint (Fig. 1) is satisfactory if the wrapping is done well. This method of attachment produces a comparatively stable board. If the board is to last very long, it must be made of a wood that is not prone to split. If there is no reinforcement where the rope passes through, the board should be at least 1 in. thick. A board of ¾-in. thickness can be used if it is reinforced with cleats similar to those shown at C and D. When cleats are used, the rope passes through both the board and the cleats.

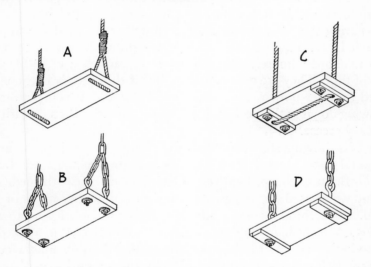

At B is shown an attachment equivalent to A except that chains and eyebolts (Fig. 2) are used. This method also produces a relatively firm board. The board should be selected with the same considerations in mind as mentioned in the discussion of A. In addition, the board may be reinforced with cleats, and if cleats are used the eyebolts are passed through both the board and the cleats.

At C is shown a method of rope attachment which results in a board that may be tilted easily forward or backward. Adventurous

23

children usually prefer this kind of board to the firmer type. It is easier to get on and it allows more graceful soaring. This method of attachment has also the advantage that there are fewer joints in the rope and no joints at the seat. It has the disadvantage that when the rope wears the whole length must be replaced.

At *D* is shown an equivalent method of attachment to *C* except that chains are used. Because it is not practical to pass chains through and under the board, eyebolts are used to attach the chains.

Fittings for Swing Ropes *(fig. 11)*

Fittings useful in the attachment of swing ropes are sketched in Fig. 11. At *A* is a rope loop formed around a thimble. The end is whipped (Introduction). At *B* is shown a factory-made steel clamp, also used for securing the short end of a loop. How it is attached to a rope can be seen in *D*. These clamps can be bought in hardware stores and from mail-order houses. They are made in various sizes to fit various sizes of rope. They are easy to attach, but if the threads become badly rusted they are not so easy to remove. Therefore, if you plan to take the swing down at the beginning of winter, coat the threads with paint or heavy grease.

At *C* is shown a steel thimble for use with rope. It is manufactured in several sizes. How it is used can be seen by looking carefully at *A* and *D*. Because cheap, lightweight thimbles will wear through rather rapidly when used on swing ropes, buy a good quality made of heavy metal. Rope thimbles are available with a plating of zinc to retard rusting. A little hard cup grease applied about once a week during the swinging season to the spot where the thimble makes contact with the bolt or hook from which it hangs will retard wear.

D shows an excellent method of attaching a swing rope to an overhead support by means of a J bolt. The threaded portion of the bolt extends through the crosspiece of the swing frame and is held by the nut and washer on top. The rope loop is first hung on the bolt, then the nut is drawn up and the unthreaded end guided into the shallow hole bored in the underside of the crosspiece. Thus the bolt is prevented from turning under the vibration of the swinging. You will

24

probably have difficulty finding bolts of this type in hardware stores, but blacksmith shops and machine shops can make them. A bolt of at least ½-in. diameter is desirable for swings.

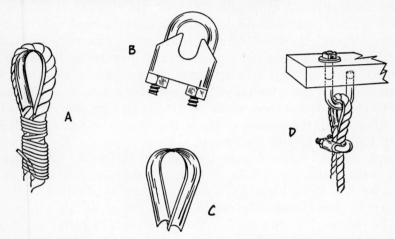

Eyebolts (Fig. 2) may also be used to hang swing ropes, but it is more difficult to install them so that they will not turn and loosen. Strongly made hammock hooks, which are available in most hardware stores, offer another method of attaching swing ropes at this point. Some porch swing hooks make excellent swing hangers, also. Bolts rather than screws are preferable for attaching the hammock or porch swing hooks to the swing frame even though rather slender bolts must be used. Most factory-made hooks of the kinds mentioned require four bolts or screws.

Chains and Fittings *(fig. 12)*

There is no single answer to the question whether rope or chain should be used to hang a swing. Both rope and chain have their advantages and disadvantages. Rope's chief disadvantage is that its length changes substantially under the influence of moisture. A swing hung on long ropes will be several inches farther from the ground on a morning after a rainy night than it will be during a period of dry

25

weather. Ropes are much more comfortable for the swinger to grasp than chain. They are never cold to the touch and they provide a more natural handhold. Chains do not swell and shrink. They will not rot if neglected, although eventually they will rust.

It is a little more difficult for persons inexperienced with rope to produce dependable joints. A sailor, for example, can make a whipped joint that is as strong as the rope itself, and if necessary he can make a spliced joint which is even stronger. A knot tied by an expert will be neat and will serve the purpose for which it is intended. The same cannot always be said for joints and knots tied by non-experts. On the other hand, the joining of chain requires some facility with the use of tools, particularly wire pliers.

Rope used to suspend swings should be preferably new rope of high quality. Although good-quality manila rope as small as ¼ in. in diameter has strength enough to support any weight that could be reasonably anticipated on a child's swing, a rope of larger diameter is to be preferred for two reasons. First, it provides a better handhold; and second, it will be safe much longer. Rope of ½-in. or even ⅝-in. diameter is recommended for swings that will be used by school-age children.

Fig. 12 A shows three links of welded steel chain. This chain is available in many sizes. The size is determined by the diameter of the wire used to make it. The ¼-in. size not only looks substantial enough for use on swings, but has the required strength many times over. Zinc-plated chain should be used in order to retard rust.

At D is shown a less expensive kind of chain. This is woven wire chain. Its strength in the common sizes is considerably less than welded chain, but it is adequately strong for swings nevertheless. The size known as 3–0 with 7½ links per foot is recommended for swings for school-age children.

At B are shown two devices useful for fastening links of chain together or attaching chain to hooks, eyebolts, etc. The top one is known as a repair link. As shown, it is split so that the chain link can be passed along the split to its center. The lower one is an "S" hook. When purchased, the two links are open as shown. If necessary, they may be hammered shut after the chain links are placed in them.

At C is shown a combination swivel snap and S hook. It is a handy gadget for attaching the chains on swings for small children, but it cannot be recommended for use on a swing that will be heavily used by larger ones. The reason is that wear will cause the short pin that permits the snap to swivel to pull away from its link with the S hook. This might not happen for a year or even longer, but when it happens the combination will come apart suddenly and without advance warning.

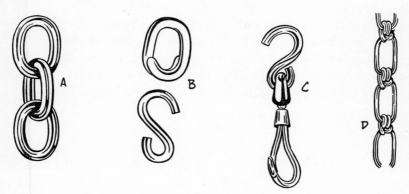

Not shown is another handy device for joining chains called a cold-shut chain repair link. It is available in various sizes from stores that sell hardware and it is inexpensive. When sold the link is partly open, but it is easily closed and riveted shut with ordinary tools.

In addition it is possible to buy porch swing chains in pairs with the branches for attaching to the arms already formed. The over-all length of these chains is about 7 ft., but the two branches at the bottom are often too long for use on board swings. However, some links can be cut off these and more links can be added to the main chain rather easily.

Lawn Swing for Children *(fig. 13)*

At one time lawn swings were as standard as front porches. In the days before every family owned a car, every family with a yard in which to place a lawn swing owned one. Then practically all of the swings were built in adult size, but the children used them—of course, at times when the adults did not want to swing. Lawn swings have

27

lost most of their popularity with adults, and many children now grow up without having enjoyed one. Nevertheless, they are still popular with all children who have access to them.

In spite of its apparent complexity, a lawn swing is easy to build. The individual pieces are small, and no difficult joints are called for. All pieces are straight except those that serve to hold the slats of the seat. Patterns for cutting out of these two irregular pieces are shown reduced in Fig. 14 A and B. To use these patterns draw them full size on lumber, then cut them out with a saw. To save time, draw on the wood only as much of the background of squares as you find necessary for reproducing the shapes of the two irregular pieces.

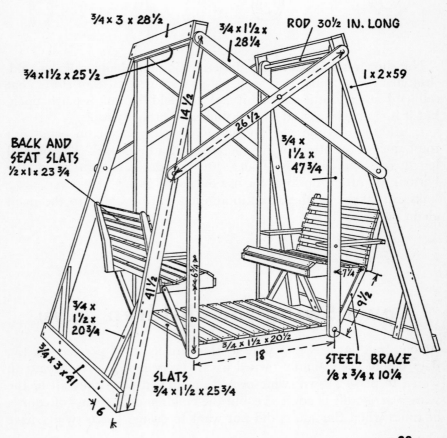

To simplify building of the lawn swing, think of it as two essentially separate units, the swinging part containing the seats and the frame from which the swinging part hangs. Build the frame, then the swinging assembly. Take care to cut like parts to the same dimensions and to center holes accurately. Avoid lumber that contains knots and splits.

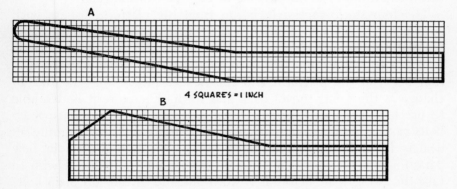

4 SQUARES = 1 INCH

As can be seen in Fig. 13, the swinging part is suspended on two rods which pass also through the main members of the stationary frame. Essentially these rods are long bolts with rounded heads on the ends visible in the drawing, and washers and nuts on the opposite ends. If steel rubs on wood at these suspension points, squeaks are almost certain to develop. To avoid this annoyance you may wish to bush the holes in the swing frame. Suitable bushings can be made of short lengths of brass pipe or copper tubing. The bushings should fit the holes in the wood rather snugly but should not be so tight that they will split the wood. A good fit between the bushing and the rod is desirable, but is not so essential as it would be in a bearing for a high-speed machine. A steel rod of ¼-in. diameter is suggested for use with bushings; without bushings use one ⅜ in. or even ½ in. in diameter.

Bushed bearings for the four bolts at the corners of the platform between the seats also are better from a mechanical standpoint than unbushed ones. However, it is doubtful whether the extra work required would be justified for a child's swing which presumably will not be used for more than a few years. Without bushings these joints will tend to squeak, but the squeaking can be reduced by placing a little cup grease between the bolts and the wood. Here the cup

29

grease can hardly drip down on anyone, whereas if it is placed in the overhead pivots it might do so.

To prevent the hangers from working toward one another along the rod on which they hang, a strip of lumber is nailed or screwed to the top of each pair. In the drawing it is placed behind the rod so as to show the rod more clearly. A better place for it is slightly below the rod on the inward side of each pair of hangers.

The four steel braces which run from the platform to the back corners of the seats have holes in them to pass the bolts that attach the platform to the hanger pieces. The nuts on the four bolts at these platform corners cannot be drawn up tight because the angular relation between the platform and the hanger pieces must be free to change as the swing moves back and forth. Therefore it is desirable to use here bolts and nuts that are designed for cotter pins. Such bolts can be obtained at some hardware stores and at practically all dealers in junk automobile parts, not to mention dealers in new parts for cars. Of course, if you are certain that you will not wish to take the swing apart before it is worn out, the threads on plain bolts can simply be battered to prevent the nuts coming off. The nuts with their cotter pins go on the inside, the heads outside.

Because the seat is rigidly attached to the hangers, the back of the seat is rigidly attached to the seat bottom, and the seat arms are rigidly attached back and front, standard carriage bolts may be used for all these joints. Lock washers (Fig. 2) under the nuts will hold them in place. Nails are used to attach the slats that form the seat bottom, seat backs, and platform. In the stationary frame all of the joints involving the crossed braces are attached with bolts, two with the long bolts or threaded rods already described, three with standard carriage bolts. Zinc-plated wood screws are recommended for all the other joints in this frame, but nails may be used instead.

The dimensions given in Fig. 13 are for a swing that will be used by children in the 3- to 8-year age range. It will accommodate at one time four children of these ages, but even one child can swing in it with ease. Except for very little ones who cannot make a big swing go, children enjoy an adult-size swing, and the construction of one is not much more difficult than the construction of this smaller version. Building of a large swing rather than a small one is suggested if your children have all reached school age. At least one of the companies in the business of publishing patterns for home woodworking projects offers a pattern for an adult-size swing.

Recommended Materials

Lumber

For all the wooden parts: No. 1 grade of a strong wood such as white pine, Southern pine, Douglas fir, and others. Consult your lumber dealer about the most economical sizes to buy from his stock for this swing.

Hardware

For attaching the slats to the platform and seats: 16-gauge 1¼-in. brads.

For various joints in the frame and swing: Zinc-plated wood screws and carriage bolts.

The special hardware, that is, the long threaded rods and the four steel braces, has been described, and dimensions have been given.

Swinging Gate (fig. 15)

There is something about a gate which makes it irresistible to children. Its true function of closing an opening interests them very little, if at all, but they immediately sense its utility as a swing. A good deal of ingenuity has been spent by designers toward designing gates in such ways that swinging is discouraged, and the truth is it is difficult to find a perch on some of the products of this effort. In contrast, here is a gate expressly designed for swinging.

The keynote of this gate is ruggedness and stability. Even the most vigorous children will have trouble knocking it apart, and even the heaviest will not cause it to sag appreciably.

If you live where the winters are cold, the post should extend into the ground far enough so that the crosspieces attached to it are below the frost line; otherwise, freezing of the ground in winter may heave them up and loosen the gate. In regions where the ground does not freeze deeper than a few inches, or at all, the post should extend about 2½ ft. into the ground.

This post should be of wood with a high degree of decay resistance, such as redwood or cypress. If these woods are not available at prices

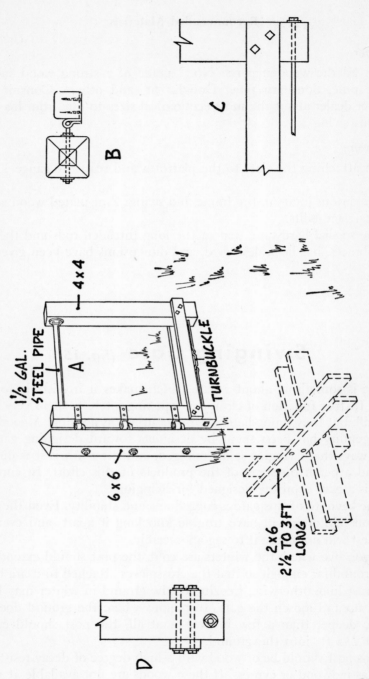

B

C

1½ GAL.
STEEL PIPE

A

4 x 4

TURNBUCKLE

6 x 6

2 x 6
2½ TO 3 FT
LONG

D

that you can afford, the post should be treated to render it decay-resistant (Introduction). The same statements apply to the cross-pieces bolted to the post. The buried crosspieces are attached to the post with carriage bolts, and the bolting should be done before the post is placed in the ground.

The gate itself is rugged not only because of the strength of its members but also because of the provisions for keeping it tight. The steel pipe at the top has floor flanges screwed to each end. These flanges may be attached to the gate frame by screws or bolts, but the latter are preferred. The two boards at the bottom of the gate are attached by carriage bolts which pass through the gate as shown in Fig. 15 D. A set of specially made rods joined by a turnbuckle are attached to the gate frame at the bottom (Fig. 15 A and C). The purpose of these is to enable occasional tightening of the gate frame when and if it shows signs of loosening. Tightening is done by drawing up the screws or bolts that secure the flanges at the top, then turning the turnbuckle.

Gate hinges similar to the ones shown in A and B can be found in some hardware stores that cater to farmers. In addition they can be made by any blacksmith. There are other types of rugged hinges which are suitable; hence, if you do not wish to have hinges specially made, show the sketch to your hardware dealer and let him suggest substitutes from his stock. It is important that the hinges be bolted to the post in such a way that the nuts can be tightened from time to time and that they allow the gate to swing both ways without binding on the post.

A good size for the gate if it is to be used by children from about 5 years to about 10 is 24 in. by 24 in. measured on the outside of the gate frame. If it is primarily for older children, 24 in. by 30 in. or even 36 in., is a more suitable size. The gate should be hung so that it will clear the ground by at least 3 in.

Recommended Materials

Lumber

For the post and buried braces: Redwood, cypress, or a construction lumber treated with a wood preservative.

For the gate frame: Any locally available lumber that is used for house framing and similar construction.

Galvanized steel pipe, 1½-in. diameter; floor flanges to fit.
Four ⅜-in. galvanized carriage bolts 6 in. long.
Four ½-in. galvanized carriage bolts 8 in. long.
Special bolts and turnbuckle as described.
Specially made hinges, or stock hinges, as described.
Galvanized wood screws or carriage bolts for hinges.

Pendulum Horse *(fig. 16)*

The pendulum horse is no spirited pony, but to a small child it may seem like one. It will always go if urged, and it is capable of carrying one or two riders.

The weight boxes that give the horse its zip are indicated by dotted lines in the drawing, and their shape is only suggested. The reason is that they should be designed to accommodate some heavy material whose total weight can be adjusted. Old-fashioned, discarded sash weights make very good ballast for this horse, and they can usually be obtained from building wreckers. However, if you cannot find them, brick or even rock will do. Appearance does not matter because the weights are concealed from view. It is important to be able to take weight off or put it on in order to adjust the horse's swing to the child.

The box concealing the weight boxes and also serving as a support for the lower bearings is designed to be concealed in the ground. It must be deep enough to allow the weight boxes to swing and provide an inch or two of extra space to permit the accumulation of some rubbish without crippling the horse. The distance of 10 in. indicated in Fig. 16 from the bearing to the bottom of the weight box is a suggestion only.

The concealed box should be made of rather heavy lumber, 1 in. in thickness or even 2 inches. Also, 2 by 4's may be used to construct it. Decay resistance in the wood (Introduction) is important if you expect the toy to last more than two seasons. The weight boxes should be made of fairly rugged material, but can be rough in appearance.

The rest of the horse should be made of rather high-grade wood, preferably some hardwood that is not too difficult to work and is not too expensive.

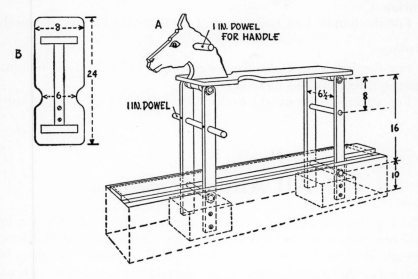

The two pairs of bearings, one under the seat, the other a couple of inches above the weight boxes, are made of short lengths of galvanized steel pipe. In the top bearings the pipe is attached to the underside of the seat with pipe hangers similar to those shown in Fig. 17 C. In the bottom bearings the pipe passes through the horse's wooden legs and through the sides of the underground box. In all joints the pipe is held in place by means of lock nuts made to fit standard pipe threads. These are available at hardware stores and plumbing supply dealers.

The board that passes between the horse's legs and serves as a cover for the box should be put on with brass screws so that it can be removed easily when cleaning of the box underneath becomes necessary.

Recommended Materials

Lumber

For the underground box: Heavy, rough lumber as described.

For the board cover: No. 1 pine or the equivalent in a locally available construction lumber ¾ in. thick.

For all other parts: A hardwood such as oak or maple, or any other locally available hardwood not too difficult to work, ¾-in. nominal thickness.

For the handle and back brace: 1-in. diameter hardwood dowels.

Hardware

For the bearings: Galvanized steel pipe, ¾-in. or 1-in. nominal diameter; hangers and lock nuts to fit.

For attaching the weight boxes: Galvanized ¼-in. carriage bolts.

All Aboard *(fig. 17)*

The toy illustrated in Fig. 17 is an uncommon one. Not quite a swing and not quite a seesaw, it combines some features of both. Children operate it by standing on the central board, grasping the pipes between the posts and "pumping." One child can work it or two can cooperate, one at each end. When more than two ride, they hold to one another's shoulders or waists.

Although it looks complicated, the device is not difficult to build. All of the woodwork is simple except for the four lapped joints, and even these can be cut with sufficient accuracy with only a saw and chisel. The dowels which pass through the lapped joints into the bottoms of the main posts are simply tapped into holes drilled through the joints and through the laps into the posts. All edges of the oscillating plank should be rounded and the plank sanded smooth and painted. The pipe frames which support the oscillating board are built of standard steel pipe and fittings.

Details of the frames are shown in Fig. 17 B and C. At the top of the frame, the horizontal pipe is not screwed to the tees, as the drawing might be interpreted. Instead, the threads are reamed out of the horizontal branches of the tees and a steel rod or pipe that fits loosely enough to allow the tees to swing is passed through the tees and the holes in the posts. This horizontal pipe or rod is drilled to receive cotter pins (not shown in the drawing). The pins keep the tees from "working" along the pipe and causing the frame to bind.

36

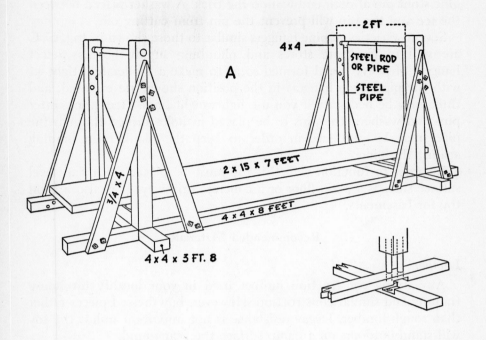

A

2 FT

4 x 4

STEEL ROD OR PIPE

STEEL PIPE

2 x 15 x 7 FEET

3/4 x 4

4 x 4 x 8 FEET

4 x 4 x 3 FT. 8

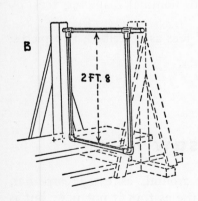

B

2 FT. 8

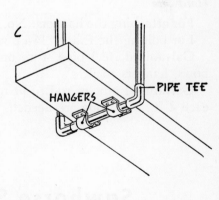

C

HANGERS

PIPE TEE

One stout pin at each end will do the trick. A washer placed between the tee and the pin will prevent the pin from cutting off.

Several varieties of pipe hangers similar to those shown in Fig. 17 C are sold in hardware stores and plumbing supply houses. Select hangers of heavy metal formed so as to make a moderately tight fit with the pipe. Two hangers in the position shown are essential, and three may be necessary if you use lightweight ones. Here also, cotter pins and washers, the pins to be placed in holes drilled through the pipe, may be necessary in order to keep the plank from binding against the pipe.

In order to function well this toy must be placed on a flat, level surface such as a patio floor or a concrete driveway. It is also a good toy for basements.

Recommended Materials

Lumber

Any strong construction lumber used in your locality for house framing and similar construction. However, buy dressed pieces rather than rough lumber. Decay resistance is not important unless the toy will stand outdoors on a damp surface the year round.

Grooved hardwood dowels, ¾-in. diameter.

Hardware

For attaching the hangers: No. 10 2-in. zinc-plated wood screws.

For bolting the frame: ¼-in. zinc-plated carriage bolts, 5 in. long.

Galvanized steel pipe, 1-in. or 1¼-in. nominal diameter; tees, elbows, hangers to fit.

Galvanized pipe or rod to fit reamed tees as described; two pieces; each 2 ft., 8 in. long are needed.

Sawhorse Seesaw *(fig. 18)*

Sawhorses are handy things to have around, as every carpenter, amateur or professional, knows. Their use as toys is not new, but is not appreciated at its full value in present-day homes, perhaps because we are too accustomed to factory-made toys of steel. No matter how you dress them up, sawhorses remain utilitarian and somewhat primitive in appearance, but this makes no difference to children.

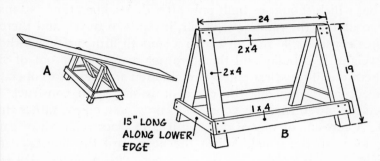

The sawhorse sketched in Fig. 18 B is a simple, lightweight one, easily carried about by children and yet sturdy enough to stand up to them. Furthermore, it is very easy to build. The only step that should give the amateur carpenter any difficulty is the cutting of the angles. This can be done easily and accurately if you have access to a carpenter's miter box. Because of the way the several parts brace one another, this sawhorse is sturdy when nailed together. Screws and bolts are not necessary.

One sawhorse is better than none, but two are more than twice as useful as one. A simple but exciting seesaw can be made with one sawhorse and a plank as shown in Fig. 18 A. Of course, the plank should be a strong and smooth one free of splinters. Two sawhorses can be used to make a bridge, or if sufficient lumber is handy, a cave or house.

Recommended Materials

Lumber

For the sawhorse: No. 2 pine or any locally available construction lumber that is moderately resistant to splintering. Dressed lumber is desirable, but not essential.

For the plank: No. 1 pine or other locally available construction lumber free of knots and splits, 2 in. by 8 in. by 8 ft. or 10 ft.

Hardware

Common nails of assorted sizes.

39

Rocking Seesaw *(fig. 19)*

Here is a basement and outdoor toy which is productive of lots of fun, but which should be built only after due deliberation. No matter how accurately the runners are built, it tends to travel, and therefore requires considerable free area with a smooth firm surface. Although lightweight, it is bulky and therefore not easy to store out of sight. Furthermore, it is useless unless two children are present to operate it.

Except for laying out the curve, it is simple to construct. The rockers are sawed from plywood. The curve is an ellipse rather than a circle. A convenient way of drawing it is to place a length of garden hose down on the panel. Adjust the hose until the line appears to be right, then trace the line on the wood with a pencil. Take care not to get the curve too flat at the center. After the first rocker has been marked and sawed out, it should be used as a guide for cutting the second one.

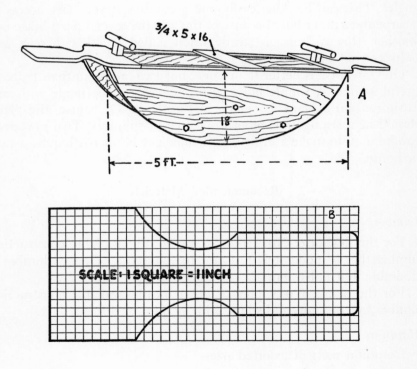

As shown in the drawing, the thickness of the rockers is increased along their top edges with boards of about 4-in. width. These boards are screwed (or bolted) to the rockers. The seats are then attached with wood screws to both the boards and the rockers.

Not shown in the drawing are three blocks placed between the rockers. These blocks are short pieces of lumber cut from either 2 by 4's or 4 by 4's. They are drilled lengthwise through their centers to pass ⅜-in.-diameter carriage bolts. In assembling the toy, each bolt is passed through a rocker, a block, and through the other rocker. Lock washers (Fig. 2) and nuts are placed on these bolts and the nuts are drawn up tight.

A plan of the seat is furnished in Fig. 19 B. By first copying the squares in their true size, then drawing in the seat outline directly on the wood, sawing of the seat will be made easy. The first seat may be used as a pattern for the second. The handles are easily made of 1-in. diameter dowel stock, a short piece of 1-in-square hardwood and a ¼-in.-diameter carriage bolt.

Rubber facings made from discarded bicycle tires are necessary for the rockers, not only to keep down noise but also to protect the edges of the plywood. Similar tires are clearly shown in Fig. 20 on another seesaw.

Recommended Materials

Lumber

For the rockers: ¾-in. exterior-type plywood.

For the seats: A splinter-free hardwood such as oak or maple, 1 in. in thickness.

For the other lumber pieces: No. 1 pine or other suitable softwood, ¾-in. nominal thickness.

For the blocks between the runners: Any wood available to you in 2-in. by 4-in. or 4-in. by 4-in. size.

Hardware

For securing the rockers: Three bolts ½ in. in diameter and 16 in. long.

For the handles: Two galvanized carriage bolts ¼-in. diameter, 5 in. long.

For other fastenings: No. 10 1½-in. galvanized wood screws.

Wheel Seesaw *(fig. 20)*

A seesaw for three is an unusual toy, as almost anyone will admit. On this seesaw (Fig. 20), the third passenger rides in the middle between the wheels. He is not essential to making the seesaw work; instead he goes along as supercargo for fun and perhaps a little piloting. For best operation this seesaw requires a firm surface underfoot such as a smooth patio floor. However, it can be operated on a level lawn in dry weather when the soil is hard, but it should not be kept long on one spot on the lawn because of possible damage to the grass.

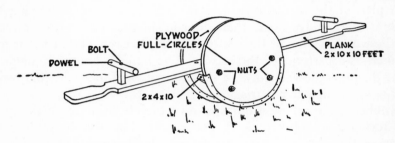

Construction is simple. The plywood circles may be sawed out of a standard 4 ft. by 8 ft. panel. In order to simplify the sawing, the panel may first be cut into two 4-ft. by 4-ft. squares. The plank is one piece of lumber and is bought in a standard size that will require no carpentry except boring of the holes for the six bolts and sawing out of the curves of the seat. Under the middle of the plank, a piece of lumber 2 in. thick, 10 in. wide, and 1 ft., 8 in. long is fastened with carriage bolts. The plywood circles also are fastened to this piece by means of long bolts passed through holes bored through it crosswise. These bolts are the upper two of the four shown on the circle in the drawing.

Lower down between the circles are placed two additional blocks cut from 2 by 4's and measuring 10 in. long. These also are bored to receive bolts, and the bolts that pass through them are the lower two of the four shown. To keep these blocks from turning, a nail or slender screw also is driven through each circle into each block.

The facings on the lower halves of the circles are necessary to protect the edges of the plywood. They also serve to keep the seesaw from being too noisy when in use. These facings are simply old bicycle

42

tires which have been cut through and opened up. The simplest way to attach them to the plywood is to nail them with aluminum brads. The brads should be spaced about 1½ in. apart along both edges.

The handles are simply constructed of standard dowel stock 1 in. in diameter, a piece about 6 in. long of lumber 1 in. by 1 in. in cross section, and a long bolt which extends downward through the plank.

If the plank is a softwood, edges should be rounded and the plank finished with an outdoor paint or varnish. While you are at it you may as well finish the rest of the structure. Color appeal may be added by painting the plank one color and the other wood in a contrasting color.

Recommended Materials

Lumber

For the circles: ¾-in. thick exterior-type plywood.
For the plank: A strong, knot-free softwood or hardwood.
For the connecting pieces under the plank and between the circles: Any strong lumber.

Hardware

For securing the plank to the piece under it: ¼-in. zinc-plated carriage bolts, 4 in. long.
For bolting the circles: Bolts ½-in. diameter, 12 in. long, zinc-plated if you can obtain them in this finish.

One-Child Seesaw *(fig. 21)*

In a good many families a seesaw that can be operated by one child is a desirable toy. This need is not necessarily limited to a one-child family. A standard seesaw requires for successful operation two children of about the same weights and approximately the same ages (so as not to get bored with one another's company). If the children in a multichild family are separated by three years or more, a standard seesaw will not get used much except when friends come to play.

The seesaw shown in Fig. 21 offers a way for a child to play without

43

waiting for a cooperative partner. Admittedly it is not as much fun for most children as a two-child seesaw when there is a cooperative playmate on the opposite end of it, but it is better than a standard seesaw without a partner to operate it.

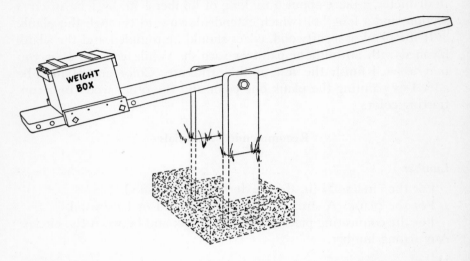

This seesaw has a weight box on one end that takes the place of the second child. The box is filled with some dense material such as brick or, better still, cast-iron sash weights. The latter can usually be purchased for a small price from dealers in used building materials or from junk dealers. When built as shown in the drawing, two adjustments are possible: (1) by adding or taking away the weights in the box, or (2) by shifting the position of the box on the plank. Instead of the arrangement shown, the box may be fastened solidly to the plank and the adjustment of balance made simply by adding or subtracting heavy material from the box. However, the sliding arrangement does not complicate the construction much. Together the two make possible very good balancing for a particular child.

Desirable dimensions for this seesaw depend upon the age of the child who is to use it most. Usually it is built for a child of pre-school age and is discarded within two or three years. For a child of about three the maximum height of the end of the plank from the ground should not be more than 2 feet. The plank itself should be 4 or 5 in. wide and have a total length of not more than 6 feet. These dimensions make a rather small seesaw, but a useful and safe one. The

44

dimensions can be increased considerably for older children. A 6-year-old, for example, will like a plank with an over-all length of about 8 ft., and a maximum rise of 3 to 3½ feet.

The box may be made of almost any lumber of ¾-in. or 1-in. thickness. It may be fastened together either with nails or with screws. The lid should be hinged and also have a fastener such as a hasp and padlock which small children cannot operate. The purpose is to keep the weights from disappearing.

Dressed lumber of 2-in. nominal thickness should be used for the plank. Holes for adjustment of the position of the box should be bored carefully so as to keep them centered between the faces of the plank. The surface should be made smooth and edges rounded. The plank should be painted or varnished to protect its surface. The plank rocks on a pipe (or rod) which passes underneath its center and is held in place by brackets or hangers similar to those shown in Fig. 17 C. There should be a gap of at least 1 in. between the plank and the upright supports on both sides to avoid pinching of small fingers. The simplest way to hold the plank away from the uprights is to slip short lengths of larger pipe over the pipe on which the plank rides. These short pieces go between the supports and the plank on both sides of the plank.

As shown in the drawing, the upright supports should be anchored in a chunk of buried concrete. For this toy the block need not be massive. Since it can be expected that the seesaw will be removed eventually, it is just as well to place the block deep. If its top is 1 ft. or more below the surface of the ground, it can be left in place after the wooden uprights are chopped away. If the seesaw is to be used for several seasons, it will be necessary to place the bottom of the concrete block a little below the frost line to avoid heaving in winter. This precaution is not necessary in regions where the ground does not freeze or freezes only shallowly. It may also be foregone if the seesaw is placed on a well drained site in gravelly or open soil.

The concrete is poured into a hole prepared for it. The uprights should be placed in the hole before the pouring or immediately afterward. They should be trued and stood parallel to each other. Temporary braces must be rigged to hold them until the concrete hardens.

Recommended Materials

Lumber

For the plank: Hardwood such as oak, or a softwood such as pine in the No. 1 grade, free of knots and splits. Dimensions have been discussed above.

For the uprights: No. 2 pine or other suitable construction wood. Treatment with a wood preservative is essential.

Hardware

For the box: Galvanized hinges, hasp, and padlock.

For holding the adjustable box: 3/8-in.-diameter bolts of suitable length.

For the pivot: 1¼-in. or 1½-in. nominal diameter steel pipe. Lock nuts and hangers to fit. Also, the two 1-in.-long pieces of galvanized pipe large enough in diameter to slip over the pivot pipe.

Steps for New Walkers *(fig. 22)*

Every small child when he is learning to walk up steps would appreciate steps of his own size. However, most children have to struggle with steps built for adults, struggle and fall, until the difficult art of climbing steps on foot is learned.

This article of play equipment (Fig. 22) is frankly a toy of limited usefulness if one measures by the term of years it will be enjoyed by one child. But the young fellow who is just learning to use his legs to ascend and descend stairs will not look at it in this way. Furthermore, if it is built as shown in the drawing, it should last for several children, if several come along.

Choice of lumber will depend partly upon where the steps are to be used. They are equally suitable for nursery, basement, or yard, but lumber that would be suitable for outdoors would not suit the nursery, though it might suit the basement. For the nursery a high-grade softwood such as No. 1 pine, free of knots, should be chosen. For outdoors or the basement, equally strong lumber should be chosen, but knots can be tolerated; that is to say, No. 2 lumber may be used. Whatever the grade, edges against which the child might fall or along which he will run his hands in using the steps or while standing on the platform should be well rounded and sanded smooth to guard against splinters.

The structure (Fig. 22) is identical on both sides; the steps going up are the same as the steps going down on the opposite side. You may wish to vary the two flights of steps by making one side as a slide. Unfortunately, the combination of steps and slide presents a hazard to the youngest walkers, although it seems to be fun for children only a little older.

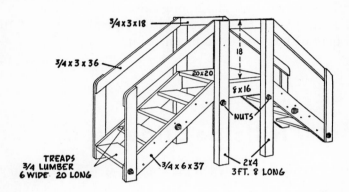

The simplest way to build this structure is to saw out and assemble the central portion with the platform first. After this is complete, the steps and railings are built and fastened to the platform. When laying out the stringers for the steps, notice that each stringer is notched at its top end to receive the edge of the platform.

Either nails or screws may be used to fasten the structure. I prefer to use No. 6 1½-in.-long wood screws to hold the treads. Spreading of the structure when it is moved about or abused is prevented by steel tie rods that run through it laterally. The nuts on the ends of these tie rods are shown in the drawing.

After it has been completely assembled, the whole structure should be finished with a non-toxic indoor paint if it is to be kept indoors, and with a non-toxic outdoor paint if it will be used outdoors.

Recommended Materials

Lumber

For all parts: The choice of lumber has been discussed above, and dimensions for the various parts are indicated on the drawing. Where the thickness is not stated on the drawing, nominal ¾-in. thickness is to be understood.

Hardware

(If the structure will be used indoors):
For the treads: Wood screws in the size given above.
For other joints: Finishing nails of suitable lengths.
For the rods: Six ⅜-in. steel bolts, 22 in. long with nuts and washers.

(If the structure will be used outdoors):
Zinc-plated screws and aluminum nails. If possible, obtain the tie rods in a zinc-plated finish; if impossible, paint them and the nuts and washers with a non-toxic metal paint.

Hillside Slide *(fig. 23)*

This device is an incredibly simple toy, yet it is amazing how much fun it is for children of all ages. It requires a hillside of appreciable slope.

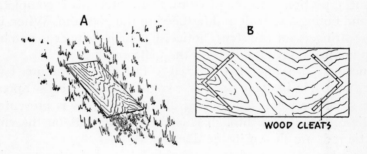

The device itself consists of nothing more than a standard 4-ft. by 8-ft. panel of ¾-in. exterior plywood with two sets of wood cleats fastened to one side. The purpose of the cleats is to keep the panel itself from being slowly propelled down the hillside by the sliding children. The cleats (Fig. 23 B) are made of lumber approximately 1 in. by 1 in. in cross section. They are fastened to the bottom of the plywood panel by a combination of water-resistant glue and wood screws. The screws must not penetrate the panel more than ½ in., hence the necessity for the glue.

48

If the panel is to get hard use, as it may if there are many children in the family or in the neighborhood, the top surface should be finished with a clear varnish designed for outdoor use. After the varnish has dried thoroughly, it may also be waxed with a paste wax. However, if the children are small and the hillside steep, omit the wax.

To use it, the panel is simply placed down on the slope (Fig. 23 A). If the cleats do not sink into the soil readily, it may be necessary to gouge out small grooves for them. The children simply sit down and slide; some will choose to roll. This slide produces one problem that I have not been able to solve: how to keep the grass alive around it. Moving the panel every day helps, but one soon runs out of hillside. Apparently it cannot be done, and one has to resign himself to seeing a brown patch developing around the panel.

A Log Pile Built to Take It *(fig. 24)*

A log pile is a good muscle builder. Children from toddlers up to high-school age like to climb over it and to sit on it. It is usually thought of as play equipment for park and school playgrounds. However, most back yards have room for at least a small one, and the logs are not as hard to obtain as some people think. In city and suburban areas where there are mature shade trees, there usually are also individuals and firms in the business of caring for them. Frequently these tree experts are called in to cut down trees which can be cut up to produce excellent logs for a child's log pile. In rural regions where there are farm woodlots, the securing of suitable logs is hardly a problem.

A good log pile must be planned and built, for a pile of loose logs can be a serious hazard, especially if the logs are stacked so that if one near the bottom rolls out the others will come tumbling down. The log pile shown in Fig. 24 is designed for safety as well as for fun. As shown in Fig. 24 A, the logs rest on a concrete slab. The slab and pile are surrounded by a shallow pit, which may be filled with sand, tanbark, or even peat moss, in order to provide a cushion for small ones who fall off the pile.

49

Loosening of the logs is prevented by passing long bolts through them. The ends of the bolts can be seen in Fig. 24 B and their positions in relation to the logs in Fig. 24 A. It can be seen also in A that the interior of the pile contains blocks of sawed lumber. As the pile is built these are inserted wherever needed in order to hold the logs in stable positions. Another purpose of the blocks is to fill chinks between logs at the end where each successive layer of logs is set back. Filling of these chinks is necessary to prevent children from getting their feet stuck between the logs.

Logs measuring from 8 in. to 1 ft. in diameter are ideal for a backyard pile. The bark must be peeled off, for it will soon wear through if it is left on. It is advisable but not essential to paint the logs with a shingle stain before the pile is assembled. The concrete slab may be omitted, but if it is the lower logs will rot within two or three seasons unless they are a decay-resistant wood. Even logs that do not rot will slowly settle into the soil. A concrete slab by itself will not stop decay of the logs altogther, but it will help, especially if it is coated with asphalt before the logs are put on it.

Theoretically the slab should extend below the frost line, but this is hardly practical in localities where the ground freezes deep in the winter, and it is not necessary in regions where there is little freezing. The slab should be located where water does not accumulate.

The natural soil should be dug out to a depth of about a foot. About 7 in. of moderately coarse gravel is then placed in the excavation and tamped. A 1:3:5 concrete mix (Introduction) is poured in to make a depth of about 3 inches. A rectangle of clean wire fencing with wires of about 9 gauge spaced not over 4 in. apart is placed on this concrete, and immediately the balance of the concrete is poured to fill the excavation.

Next, the top surface is smoothed by troweling it with a steel trowel. The surface should be sloped slightly to drain off the rain water. Once the troweling is done, the slab should be covered with building paper or hay or almost any other cheap material that will hold moisture. The covering material is kept damp for about 48 hours and then is removed.

For the coating buy an asphalt roofing cement without fibers. The cement should be the kind which may be applied cold. The asphalt is spread over the slab evenly so that no concrete shows through. The slab is then ready for the logs.

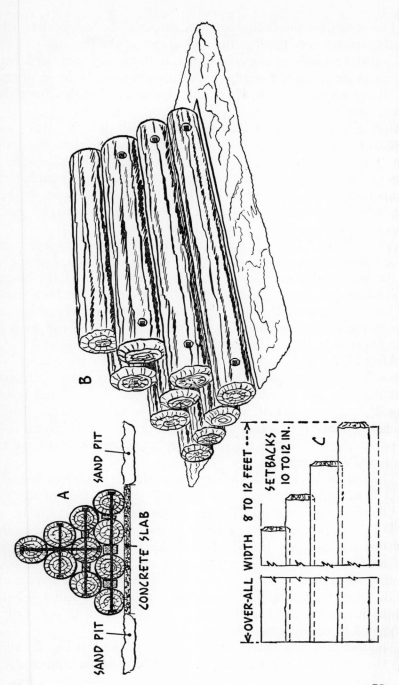

A

SAND PIT

SAND PIT

CONCRETE SLAB

B

OVER-ALL WIDTH 8 TO 12 FEET

SETBACKS
10 TO 12 IN.

C

The length of the bolts that pass through the logs is determined by the diameters of the logs themselves, hence the logs must be piled up with the blocking material between them and measured before the bolts are ordered. For a back-yard log pile bolts ¾ in. in diameter should be strong enough. Each bolt should be threaded for nuts at both ends.

Boring the holes is a tedious and difficult job for most home mechanics. I know of no more practical technique than the following: The first layer of logs is lined up with the blocking between the logs on the concrete slab and held securely by means of boards tacked temporarily across the ends of the logs. For bolts of ¾ in. diameter, the holes should be at least 1 in. in diameter. A powerful electric drill or a hand brace may be used to do the boring.

After the first hole is through the first log, drill the companion hole through the opposite end of the same log. Then, holding one of the bolts horizontally in the hole, tap it so as to mark the blocking next to the log. After the positions of both holes have been marked in this way, remove the first log without disturbing the others and repeat the boring and marking. It takes care to keep the successive holes horizontal, but it can be done.

After all the logs and blocking of the first layer have been bored through, the assembly is put back on the slab, the bolts are inserted, and the nuts are drawn up but not tightened. The second layer of logs is placed on the first, and the blocking is fitted between the logs. Then the boring operation is repeated. After the second layer is bolted together, the two logs of the third layer are placed on them and they are bored and bolted.

The fourth layer consists of only a single log. The two bolts that hold it run vertically downward between the two logs of the third layer and through the middle log of the second layer as can be seen in Fig. 24 A. Theoretically, in order to make a very stable pile, these bolts should also pass through the blocking between the two logs in the middle of the first layer. Doing so would really complicate the bolting operation, and it is unnecessary if the logs are approximately of the sizes suggested. The weight of six such logs will hold them solidly in place against all the forces a log pile would ordinarily be subjected to in children's play.

The bolt holes are bored vertically through the first log. By adjusting the lengths of the blocking—which need not be continuous be-

52

tween any of the logs—boring through any blocks for this bolt can be avoided. With the first log in place, a bolt is passed through the holes and brought to rest on the middle log of the second layer from the bottom. It is tapped to mark the log below, and this marking is repeated for the second hole.

Next, the top log is lifted off the pile; the two logs of the third layer are unbolted and lifted off; then the two holes are bored through the middle log of the second layer. These holes should go all the way through this log, but not through the blocking.

Next, the second layer of logs is unbolted and lifted off. The two vertical rods are then passed upward through the holes in the middle log of this layer. The nuts are screwed onto the rods, and then the nuts are jammed in the holes by driving nails beside them in such positions that the nails will prevent the nuts from turning.

With the vertical rods protruding, the log pile is now rebuilt layer by layer. The top log is handled carefully so as to avoid forcing the vertical rods down. As soon as this log is in place on the pile with the rods through it, the nuts are put on it and drawn up snug but not made tight. Next, the horizontal rods in the second and third layers are drawn tight, and finally the nuts on the vertical rods are made as tight as seems necessary.

The holes over the nuts in the topmost log should be filled not only for appearance, but also to keep rain water from following the bolts downward into the pile. The best method of filling is to use round wooden plugs which are secured in place by gluing with a waterproof glue. An alternative method is to fill the holes with a mixture of sawdust and waterproof glue. For appearance' sake, the holes over the nuts in the sides of the logs should also be filled, but doing so makes an unnecessary complication when the time comes to take the log pile apart. For this reason, simply painting the nuts and bolt ends with a metal paint that will retard rusting is recommended.

The ends of the logs are chamfered as can be seen in Fig. 24 B. This is done before the logs are put together, and the best tool is a sharp hatchet or a hand ax. The setback (Fig. 24 C) is usually built at only one end of the pile.

A Simpler Log Pile *(fig. 25)*

This log pile is not so elaborate, and in most locations it would not prove so durable as the log pile shown in Fig. 24, but it is much easier to build. First, fewer logs are required; second, there is no concrete slab; third, and most important, the long bolts are not necessary. Both ends go straight up; in other words there is no setback. The logs should be peeled and for appearance' sake they should be painted with an attractive shingle stain. (Do not, however, expect the stain to protect the logs against rot, especially those logs in contact with the soil.)

The steel strapping used to hold the logs is the flexible type, commonly used for binding shipping boxes. It and the lag screws can be purchased at hardware stores. Lag screws should be long enough to penetrate the logs about 2 in., and should be at least ½ in. in diameter. The stakes are best made of 2 by 4 lumber and they will last longer if treated with a wood preservative (Introduction) before they are driven into the ground.

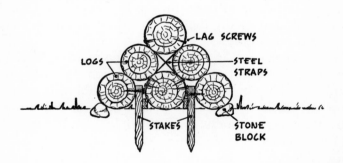

The pile is constructed as follows: The outer logs of the first layer are put in place and blocked with stone. Stakes are then driven against them. There should be at least 3 stakes along each log. After the stakes are well driven, they are bored and lag screws long enough to penetrate the logs at least 2 in. are screwed through them and into the logs. The center log is placed next, and blocking is driven between it and the stakes as shown. At least three pairs of straps should be planned, crossed as shown in the figure, and each strap should be attached to the middle log by one or two lag screws.

After the holes have been bored in the logs for the screws, the straps are marked and holes are drilled through them to pass the

54

screws. Next, the lower ends of the straps are fastened to the log by means of the lag screws which are turned up tight. The logs of the second layer are placed next, and the straps bent back over them and tacked down temporarily.

The top log is placed in position, and positions are marked for the lag screws. (These screws should, of course, be placed where they will be out of the way of climbers on the pile. The position shown in the figure is about right.) The log is turned over and the holes are drilled for the screws. Next, it is turned back to its final position and the straps are bent around it and marked for drilling. The log is removed again, and the straps are drilled for the lag screws.

Finally the log is placed back, the straps are brought one by one into position and fastened with the screws. Any excess length of strap is cut off with a hack saw or chisel, and the rough edge is turned over with a blunt chisel. If the top log is loose after all the screws have been fastened, make it tight by driving wedges between it and the adjacent logs. Good wedges can be made from scrap shingles.

As a final operation, look over the pile for any chinks in which small feet might be caught. Fill any that seem hazardous with blocking made from scrap lumber and nail the blocking in place.

Jumping-off Place *(fig. 26)*

From the age of two upward to the high-school age, most children enjoy jumping. Country children can usually find a fence or a stone wall, or a beam in the barn, but children living in cities or suburban areas often have nothing to jump from but flights of steps, and these are most unsatisfactory. The plaything shown here will probably not benefit city children, but I hope that it will give pleasure to many living in the country and the suburbs.

Although it is somewhat easier to build it on a hilly site, it can be constructed on a level spot. The small hills that lead up to it can be mounds of soil covered with turf. The section view (Fig. 26 A) shows the construction. Two or three substantial posts whose lower ends are buried in the soil support the face pieces. The sole function of the face pieces is to hold the soil behind them in place.

The part labeled "sand pit" need not be filled with sand, but it is a good idea to make a hollow about a foot deep in the natural soil and to remove all such objects as stones and roots. It may be filled with peat moss, straw, or tanbark if you can get it. The requirements are that the material be springy and remain so in spite of the weather.

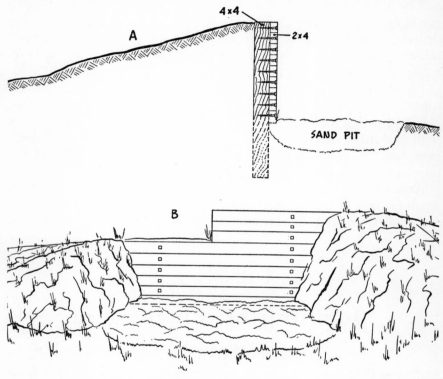

There are no best dimensions for this structure. In Fig. 26 B it is shown with two steps or heights. The purpose is, of course, to provide a low place for small jumpers and a higher place for bigger ones; but if the children who will use it are all 4 years old and older, one height may serve. A reasonable height for the lower portion is 2 ft. measured from the surface of the sand to the top. The other step is one foot higher, that is, 3 ft.

As sketched in Fig. 26 A, the structure is made of standard lumber pieces. Unless you use a decay- and termite-resistant wood, the 4 by 4's should be treated throughout their lengths with a wood preservative before the structure is erected. Decay resistance is desirable also in the horizontal pieces, but is not quite so essential because of the relative ease of replacing them. The lag screws should be long enough to go through the 2 by 4's and penetrate the 4 by 4's at least 2 inches.

Lumber in the dimensions just cited makes a rather light structure in comparison to one that may be made of such pieces as railroad ties. Discarded railroad ties are available in many localities. They are usually somewhat decayed and full of splinters. Nevertheless, if you have the opportunity to sort over a considerable pile, you can probably find enough to build this structure. Splinters can be removed and rough spots made relatively smooth by a little work with chisel and plane. The best faces of the ties should be placed outward.

Because railroad ties are approximately 8 in. by 8 in. in cross section, rather long screws will be needed. In addition, drilling the holes and running the screws in will be more laborious. On the other hand, railroad ties have usually been treated with a wood preservative, and most old ties still retain considerable decay resistance.

Boxes for Play *(fig. 27)*

A strange thing about boxes as playthings is that their value is realized by the specialists who select play equipment for nursery schools, but few parents provide them for home play. Perhaps the reason is that boxes are not sold as playthings in stores. Children, especially children of kindergarten age, enjoy boxes almost as much as any other kind of toy.

Fortunately for parents interested in making toys for their children, strong boxes are easy to make. A method of construction that results in a box able to withstand playground use for a long time is illustrated in Fig. 27. A completed box is shown at B and the frame of the box at A. A square, a saw, and a hammer are all the tools needed to make this box, and although it is somewhat stronger when put together with screws, it is strong enough when fastened with nails.

Although small children enjoy boxes that can be sat in, a box that is closed all around is more useful for standing on and for making structures. The skeleton shown at A is not used as such, but is converted into a closed box by nailing plywood pieces of appropriate sizes between frame members. Plywood that is thinner than the frame members produces a box which has convenient handholds. By using wood that has the same thickness as the frame members, boxes that are essentially smooth can be made.

A

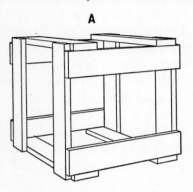

B

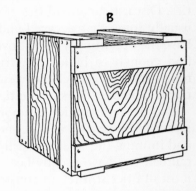

Dimensions for boxes of this kind vary according to the ages of the children and the kind of play they are intended for. If the children are young and the object is to encourage building, the boxes should be of various sizes, but none should be too large. On the other hand, boxes that are to be stood on or used to hold up planks can be larger because the children will not need to lift them high. Almost any size from cubes 1 ft. on a side up to 1½ ft. by 2 ft. by 3 ft. can be handled by children in the 4- to 7-year age range. Only the smaller boxes should be perfect cubes. As the dimensions increase, the height and width of the box should decrease relative to its length. To illustrate: a box measuring 15 in. by 15 in. by 15 in. is a useful toy, but a box 3 ft. by 3 ft. by 3 ft. would be very inconvenient to play with.

Recommended Materials

Lumber

For the box frame: Any locally available softwood that is reasonably strong and fairly light in weight. Recommended thickness, ¾ in.; and recommended widths, 2½ in. or 3 in.

For the panels between the frame members: ⅜-in. exterior-type plywood. Board lumber may also be used, but unless carefully chosen it will make boxes that are too heavy.

Hardware

For nailing the frame: 6-penny box nails.

For nailing plywood of ⅜-in. thickness: 3-penny box nails. Aluminum nails will not rust, but consider whether their extra cost is justified in a toy of this kind.

Through and Over *(fig. 28)*

Here is a toy that is productive of much fun. It consists of a large tile, two flights of steps, and a platform. It may be jumped from, crawled through, and climbed. Discarded railroad ties were mentioned earlier as a building material for the construction of another play device. They are even more suitable for this one. The dimensions of railroad ties are not fixed, but 8 in. by 8 in. is a typical cross section. For this toy they may have to be sawed off so that their lengths match that of the tile, but they should not require much other work except rounding of corners and cutting away of splinters.

Both the tile and the first layer of ties may be placed directly on the soil. If the spot is grassy, it is well to remove the grass and the top 4 to 6 in. of soil before putting them down. After the site has been prepared, the tile (or two tiles if you wish a longer tunnel) is placed on the soil and a tie is pushed up snug against it on each side. The remainder of the first layer of ties is then put down. The second layer is placed on it, beginning with the ties next to the tile and working outward. Spikes are driven through the corners of these ties into the ties below as shown in Fig. 28 B. This process is repeated with the next layer and so on until the next to the top row is reached. Boards are placed crosswise of the next-to-the-top row of ties, and the platform is constructed on the top row. All of the boards are nailed to the ties under them.

After the structure is built, stones and soil or soil alone are banked against its ends (Fig. 28 A) in such a way that both the tile and the ties are held from moving laterally. Soil between the ties and tile inside the structure is optional. The mounds of earth may be turfed if you wish them to look green.

59

A

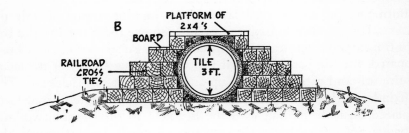

B

PLATFORM OF
2 x 4 's

BOARD

RAILROAD
CROSS
TIES

TILE
3 FT.

Lumber

For the platform: 2-in. by 6-in. lumber of any species used locally for house framing and similar construction.

For the main structure: Discarded railroad ties.

For the hollow center: One or two concrete sewer tiles. Select tiles with fairly smooth interiors.

Hardware

Common nails and spikes of appropriate lengths.

Obstacle Box *(fig. 29)*

Some adults have difficulty seeing anything that is exciting about this device, but children of the kindergarten age and also those a year or two younger and a year or two older find it very interesting. The device is a simple one, easy to make and also easy to move. It can be taken into the garage and stood against a wall during the winter, or, if there is room, into the basement where it will be played in with the same interest as when it is outdoors.

Construction of this toy, therefore, should start with acquisition of a ladder, either an old ladder or a new one. The main point is to pick a ladder with rungs that are smooth. The frame on which the ladder sections rest is easily made of common lumber. The ladders are secured to the frame with iron straps as shown in Fig. 29 A and B. The straps pass over the ladder rungs and are fastened with screws or nails to the frame. One ladder section is raised at one end and is mounted on the main frame. This block may be joined to the main frame with iron plates and wood screws as shown in Fig. 29 B, or it may be held with dowels.

Over-all dimensions depend somewhat upon the dimensions of the ladder used. The dimensions included in the sketch are suggested ones only. The frame should be made wide enough so that there is a middle passageway of 12 to 18 in. between the two ladder sections.

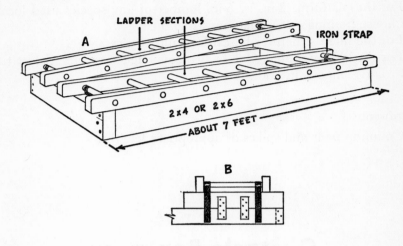

Recommended Materials

Lumber

For the frame: Any locally available construction lumber.

Hardware

For attaching the ladders to the frame: Flexible steel straps, about 1 in. wide. Galvanized preferred. Sharp edges should be turned under.

For attaching the elevated block to the main frame: Iron plates ⅛ in. by 2 in. by 4 in.

Climbing Gym *(fig. 30)*

A full-size climbing gym such as is often seen in school playgrounds costs some hundreds of dollars and is not a toy that the average father would rush to buy, even though children are drawn to this equipment as to a magnet. Fortunately, it is possible to build at home satisfactory substitutes. If you have good luck in picking up the pipe at dealers in used building supplies and can get lumber that is moderate in price, the climbing gym shown in Fig. 30 need not empty your pocketbook. Furthermore, it is not necessary to make one as elaborate as the one shown if you are interested in economy.

All of the upright members of this gym are 4-in. by 4-in. posts, and all of the horizontal members are steel pipe. Only galvanized pipe should be used. The 1-in. nominal diameter is adequately strong, but the 1¼-in. or 1½-in. sizes will give the structure a more substantial look. The choice may be determined by the size of pipe you can purchase at a reasonable price. Because it is next to impossible to find used lumber free enough of nails and splinters, the lumber must be new. However, it need not be the most expensive wood available. Wood that is full of knots should be avoided; otherwise, it can be almost any construction lumber available in the 4 in. by 4 in. size.

This device should not stand on a concrete base in spite of the fact that you sometimes find similar play equipment standing on concrete in public playgrounds. A well drained spot should be chosen and made level. The 4 by 4's simply stand on the soil; that is to say, they are not buried in it. Because they do stand on the soil their lower 6 in. should be treated with a wood preservative before the structure is built.

Building proceeds as follows: The lumber is looked over and rough spots, splintery patches, etc., are cut out or smoothed. The upright pieces are cut to length. The holes for the pipes are bored. Sharp corners are planed off, then rounded by sanding. The pipes are cut to length.

The shorter rows of posts are assembled one at a time. First, four of them are laid down with the sides uppermost that will be on the outside in the completed structure. They are spaced approximately right, then the pipes are run through them horizontally. With the pipes in place, holes are drilled in the two outer posts and also in the

63

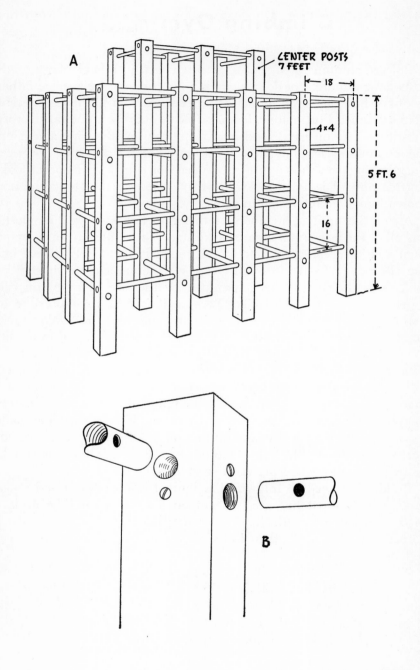

A

CENTER POSTS
7 FEET

⊢—— 18 ——⊣

4×4

5 FT. 6

16

B

ends of the pipe to receive the screws that lock the pipes into the posts (Fig. 30 B). This whole procedure is repeated for each successive row of uprights until all have been assembled.

Next, the last row of posts assembled is stood up on the spot it will occupy and the top and bottom pipes at both ends are started through it at right angles to the pipes already in place. When these pipes have been pushed through so that about 18 in. of each is projecting, the next row of uprights is stood up and the pipes are pushed forward into the appropriate holes in it. This procedure is repeated until all of the rows are standing horizontally. Insertion of the in-between pipes and of the pipes in the tower follows.

When all the pipes are in place, drill the holes in the end posts for the other locking screws and get them in place. Once the pipes are fixed in the eight end posts, the interior posts should be accurately spaced. A wooden mallet is a handy tool for tapping them into place. Locking screws are needed only at the ends of pipes. At other points, drive in thin wooden wedges between the pipe and the wood of the post.

For greatest attractiveness, the wood in this structure should be finished with a shingle stain or exterior paint. It is a good idea to do the painting before the parts are put together even though some retouching will be necessary afterward.

Simpler Climber *(fig. 31)*

This climbing apparatus is considerably simpler than the one described in the preceding article, and it takes less room in the yard. It lacks some of the maze-like quality of the more elaborate structure; but on the other hand, when dimensioned as shown in Fig. 31 it offers more challenge to adventurous climbers because of the greater distances between bars. When built in the dimensions suggested on the drawing, it is suited for average children above the ages of 7 or 8. Of course, it can be built with the same spacings between the horizontal members and the vertical ones as are suggested for the more elaborate apparatus described in the preceding article. If built smaller, however, it will not be interesting to sophisticated climbers.

65

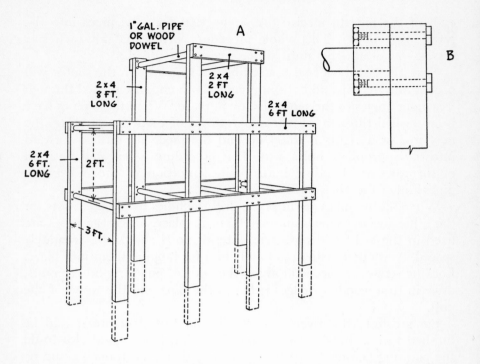

Because of its small base, this structure must be anchored to something at the bottom. It is possible to make a wooden base for it by nailing 2 by 4's or 2 by 6's about 10 feet long crosswise of the pairs of uprights where they rest on the ground. This is perhaps the best kind of base when it is known that the structure will have to be taken down soon or moved, but it does give the equipment a temporary, unartistic appearance that does not suit a well kept yard. Everything considered, the preferable method of anchoring is to dig a post hole about 18 in. deep in the ground for each of the uprights. If the site is well drained, it should not be necessary to go deeper even though the ground freezes deeper in the winter. If the soil is a dense clay that drains poorly, it should be excavated and the site filled with a more open soil or even gravel. I do not recommend a concrete base because of the hazard it presents when a child falls.

Galvanized steel pipe is recommended for the round horizontal members of this structure. On a cool day the steel pipe will be cold to the touch, but you can be sure that it will not be attacked by termites

66

or rot or develop a split. Carefully selected used pipe should serve as well as new. If you prefer to use wood for these parts, get it in a generous diameter. Standard hardwood dowels are seldom available in a diameter larger than one inch. However, closet hanger rods are often available in larger diameters and are carried in stock by most lumber yards that cater to house builders. Long pieces of adequate diameter can also be turned from stock lumber if you have a woodworking lathe or one of your friends has one.

The horizontal rods are joined to the wood with a joint that is both simple and adequately strong. As shown in Fig. 31 B, the pipe or rod rests in a hole bored through the vertical post, but does not penetrate the 2 by 4 that is bolted to it and runs horizontally. The two timber pieces are joined with four carriage bolts.

A simple way to erect this structure is to treat each one of the long sides as a separate frame of identical measurements. Each is built completely. The 10 rods, or pieces of pipe, are cut to identical lengths.

The holes are dug and the frames are raised to an upright position and stood in them. All of the lengths of pipe are inserted, working upward from the bottom row. Be sure to have a stepladder on hand to use when putting in the top ones. After the pipe is all in place, the two frames are drawn toward one another and held firmly by two or three boards temporarily nailed across from one side to the other. Finally, the frame is made plumb and the post holes are filled with concrete or with gravel. If concrete is used, no force should be applied to the structure either vertically or horizontally until the concrete has set firmly, and the gym should not be used for play for two or three days.

If the structure seems a little wobbly at the top after the post holes have been packed with gravel, or if concrete was used, after it has become firm, put in a few metal tie rods. A good position for them is directly under the horizontal pipes. They should pass entirely through the wood on both sides and be threaded at both ends to receive bolts and washers.

Recommended Materials

Lumber

For the frame: No. 2 pine or its equivalent in locally available construction lumber.

For the climbing bars (if you choose to use wood): Closet hanger rod of 1½-in. diameter or larger, or custom-made rods of similar diameter. These rods should be entirely free of knots and other defects that might affect their strength. (If you choose steel): 1¼-in. or 1½-in. diameter galvanized steel pipe.

Hardware

Galvanized carriage bolts, ¼-in. diameter and 4 in. long. Steel tie rods of ½-in. diameter if needed.

Horizontal Ladder *(fig. 32)*

Here is a piece of equipment loved by boys from 5 years to at least 16 years old. Girls will use it also if given the opportunity. In the heights suggested on Fig. 32, it is not tall enough for 16-year-olds who are 6 ft. tall; but it will suit boys of average height of this age. If the one you make is to be made for tall boys, increase the recommended height by 1½ to 2 ft. However, do not make it so tall for small boys. If the surface beneath the horizontal ladder is soil or turf, there is little risk of a boy's being hurt if he drops from underneath the horizontal ladder; but adventurous boys will get on top and walk across. A fall from on top could cause injury.

The easiest way to build this structure is to shop for some ladders with approximately the right dimensions. Three straight ladder sections will be needed. It will be necessary to modify them somewhat, but even so, buying ladder sections rather than making them from scratch should save much time and trouble.

Extra rungs in the factory-made ladders should be removed by sawing them off or by boring out their ends where they come through the ladder sides, then punching them out. Three or four rungs may have to be removed at the top of the sections placed vertically. Alternate rungs are removed from the ladder section that is used horizontally in the structure, and here, sawing off the rungs so as to leave the holes filled is the better technique. The lower ends of the sections

68

that will be placed in the ground should be treated with a wood preservative. The steel braces are ⅛-in. or ¼-in. steel straps obtainable at some hardware stores and from blacksmith shops. Carriage bolts are used to join the ladders at the top and to attach the steel braces.

So much stress is put on a structure of this kind by a few husky boys that it is necessary to anchor it firmly, hence the concrete around the posts. The holes for ends of the ladder sections are dug about 1 ft. square and about 2 to 2½ ft. deep. A flat piece of stone or concrete block is placed levelly in the bottom of each to hold the ends of the ladders temporarily. After the structure is fully assembled, the ladders are stood in the holes and a 1:3:5 concrete mix (Introduction) is

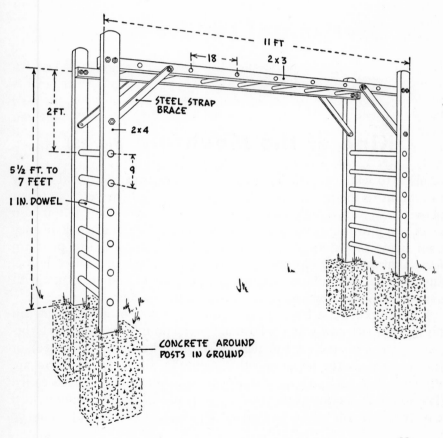

poured around them. The structure should be made plumb before the concrete is placed, and as soon as the pouring is completed the structure should be tested again for plumbness and adjusted if necessary. Braces to hold it in place while the concrete sets are a reassuring safeguard, but if children can be kept from testing the equipment for 48 hours braces may not be necessary.

Recommended Materials

Lumber

Three factory-made ladder sections of appropriate heights.

Hardware

Steel straps ⅛ in. or ¼ in. thick, 1¼ in. or 1½ in. wide. Paint them with a good outdoor metal paint to retard rusting.

¼-in.-diameter zinc-plated carriage bolts of appropriate lengths.

King of the Mountain *(fig. 33)*

A place to which he can climb and look out over the world is very important to the growing child. Not only does a high perch put him above the heads of adults who usually tower over him, but it also gives him a feeling of conquering his environment. The article of play equipment shown in Fig. 33 serves as a tower, and the platform located at midpoint also makes a kind of substitute for a tree house. In fact, it is not difficult to line the interior of the structure with canvas walls and thus convert it into a teepee or cave.

The structure can be built as a permanent one or as one that can be taken apart and stored. To make it demountable, the joints between the ladders and the platforms must be bolted, screwed, or hooked. Hooks for the frame that supports the larger platform are shown in Fig. 33 B. These permit this platform to be removed easily. The joints at the top platform may be made with the common steel corner braces or with stepladder brackets. Construction can be

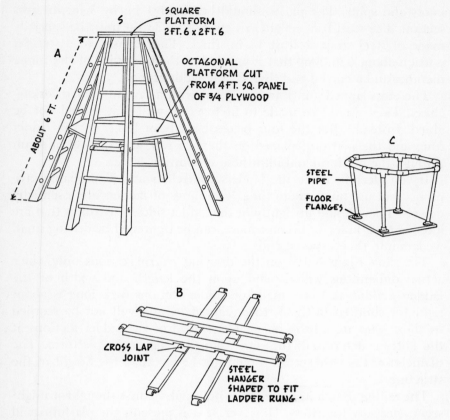

S

SQUARE PLATFORM 2 FT. 6 x 2 FT. 6

OCTAGONAL PLATFORM CUT FROM 4 FT. SQ. PANEL OF ¾ PLYWOOD

A

ABOUT 6 FT.

C

STEEL PIPE

FLOOR FLANGES

B

CROSS LAP JOINT

STEEL HANGER SHAPED TO FIT LADDER RUNG.

simpler if demountability need not be built in. The top platform would still be attached with corner braces or stepladder brackets, but a simple wood frame nailed or screwed to the sides of the ladders would hold the larger platform.

Construction is simplified considerably if you can get hold of four stepladders. Tall stepladders of the kind used by house painters usually have flared ladder sections which are just right. In addition, in most cases the top end of the ladder is attached with a bracket which will serve very well in attaching it to the top platform of this equipment.

Both the small top platform and the larger platform may be sawed from one 4-ft. by 8-ft. panel of ¾-in. plywood. The frame that supports the larger platform should be made of lumber which is free of knots and splits. The pieces should be about 1 in. by 3 in. in cross section. The steel hangers at their ends (Fig. 33 B) must be specially made of steel strap at least ¼ in. thick. They consist of a straight portion about 6 in. long that is screwed to the underside of the frame member and a curved end that fits the ladder rung.

The cross-lapped joints are easily cut with a saw and woodworking chisel. They should be made to fit together well, but should not be glued. Instead, after the four pieces have been hung on the ladder rung and the platform placed on them, a few wood screws are run through the platform and into these supporting pieces.

If you elect to make the ladders yourself, you will probably save money but use much more time. The rungs of ladders are essentially dowels. They should fit tightly in the ladder sides. Any rungs that are loose in their holes, or become loose, can be tightened by driving small wedges into their exposed ends.

The dimensions noted on the drawing are suggestions only, since actual dimensions will depend upon the length and width of the ladder sections. A tower made of ladder sections 6 ft. long is about right for children in the 5- to 8-year range, and will not be scorned by those who are a little older. The spread of the ladder sections at the bottom determines the dimensions of the larger platform. The diameter of the base spread should not be less than the height of the structure.

The railing shown in Fig. 33 C is optional. At first thought it might seem necessary for safety. However, if it is present, the platform will be more difficult to get onto, and once a climber has reached it he can fall about as easily over the railing as off the platform without a railing. A railing offers the most protection against falling on occasions when two or more children are on the platform simultaneously.

Recommended Materials

Lumber

For the ladder sections: Factory-made ladder sections of stepladders.

For the platforms: ¾-in. exterior-type plywood.

For the supports for the larger platforms: No. 1 pine or other strong first-grade lumber at least 1 in. by 3 in. in cross section.

Hardware

For supporting the larger platform: Specially-made steel strap hangers as described above.

For attaching the platforms: Galvanized wood screws or galvanized carriage bolts of appropriate lengths.

For construction of the railing: Standard steel pipe and fittings, ¾-in. or 1-in. nominal diameter.

Chinning Bar I *(fig. 34)*

A chinning bar has a stronger appeal for the high-school-age group than for any other. However, younger children, especially boys, will make use of one if it is available. In building a chinning bar for the use of a family, it is just as well to make it sturdy so that father may demonstrate his strength on it too. The structure shown here (Fig. 34) can be used for other acrobatics as well as for chinning. It can even be used to support a swing, but if there is room in the yard for a separate swing it is advisable to provide one.

This structure should be made sturdy. A cross section of 4 in. by 4 in. is the minimum for the posts, and 6 in. by 6 in. is preferable. The best height depends upon the height of those who will use it. A man 6 ft. tall with average arm length will want the bar at about 8 ft. On the other hand, a boy who is 4½ ft. tall will need the bar placed at about 5½ ft. If smaller children are going to try the apparatus, the lowest position of the bar should be suited to their reach. Fortunately, it is not difficult to provide for adjustments over a considerable range of the bar's height.

As shown in the sketch, holes are bored through both posts to accommodate the bar at various heights. To make the best adjustments for small children, these holes should be placed 4 in. center to center. For older children and adults, a 6-in. spacing is usually satisfactory. The holes should be made large enough so that the bar can be moved easily. The pipe is held in the hole by means of a pin inserted through a hole in the pipe as shown in Fig. 34 B. This pin is easily made by cutting the point off a large spike.

73

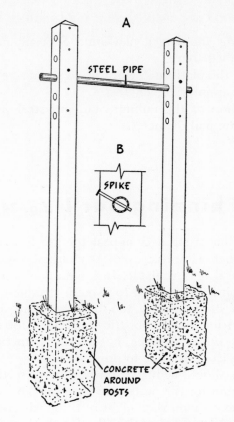

Unless the site is unusually well drained and the soil a firm type, some concrete around the posts is advisable as shown in Fig. 34 A. The holes should be made about a foot square and the posts centered in them, surrounded by the concrete. How deep to make the holes will depend upon how stable you wish the structure to be and how deep the ground freezes in winter. In regions of deep freezes, in order to avoid misalignment of the posts, the holes should be dug to a few inches below the frost line. If the frost line is not deep in your locality, a depth of 2 ft. should be adequate except in very loose soil.

Recommended Materials

Lumber

Redwood or cypress 6 in. by 6 in. If these woods are unobtainable, pine or other strong wood will serve if the length to be buried in the concrete and about 6 in. more are well treated with a wood preservative (Introduction).

Hardware

A smooth length of galvanized steel pipe, 1¼ in. or 1½ in. in diameter.

Chinning Bar II *(fig. 35)*

The chinning bar shown in this figure is not so versatile as the one described in the previous article. It cannot be used to support a swing, for example. On the other hand, it is extremely simple to build and it can be placed on the side of the garage or in some other spot where it will be inconspicuous. It is not adjustable (except by moving the whole device) and therefore is more suited to use by a group of children in the middle and late teens rather than by a family varying considerably in height and reach.

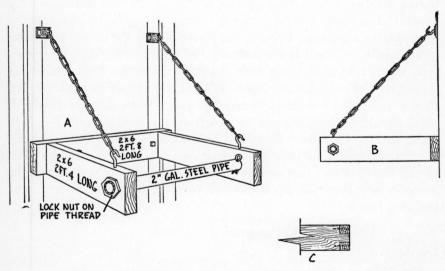

Because it is not readily adjustable, the height of the horizontal bar from the ground should be settled on only after careful measurement of the reach of the boys and girls who are going to use it. Although a steel pipe of 2-in. nominal diameter is indicated on the drawing, this diameter should be considered the maximum. In fact, a pipe of 1½-in. or 1¼-in. nominal diameter is to be preferred if the youths for whom the chinning bar is built have small hands.

The framework is easy to build. Ordinarily it would all be cut from the same piece of lumber. Accurate location of the holes for the bar is made certain by clamping the side pieces together and boring through both. The joints between the back piece and the side pieces can be made in several ways. A cross section of a joint made by a simple method is shown in Fig. 35 C. The screws indicated by dotted lines in this joint are optional. If they are used, rather slender (not larger than No. 8) flat-headed wood screws should be used, and the holes pre-drilled for them.

After the three frame pieces are joined, the pipe that forms the horizontal bar is inserted in the holes and is marked for the cotter-pin holes (Fig. 35 A). These holes should be placed so that the pins will fit snugly against the wood, for if a really snug fit is obtained at these points the steel pipe will act as a rigid member of the frame.

A coarse welded chain having 10 or 12 links per foot looks better than a smaller chain, although practically any welded chain sold for general utility use will have the necessary strength. In the drawing screw hooks are shown holding the lower end of the chain and hammock hooks or porch hooks holding the upper end. Actually, either type may be used at both ends. In some localities hardware stores do not regularly stock screw hooks in the large diameters required, but they always have hammock hooks and porch hooks. Screw hooks, if used, should be long enough to penetrate the wood about 2 inches. Since 4 screws are used to attach hammock hooks or porch hooks, the screws for them may be a little shorter. The lag screws that attach the back member of the frame to the building wall should be placed where they will intersect studs or other heavy members of the building frame.

Recommended Materials

Lumber

No. 2 pine or other locally available construction lumber.

76

Hardware

For the bar: Galvanized steel pipe 1¼-in., 1½-in., or 2-in. nominal diameter.

For the chain: Welded steel chain with long links.

To attach the chain: Standard zinc-plated hammock hooks or porch hooks, or ¼-in. screw hooks, 3½ in. long.

To attach the frame to the wall: Zinc-plated lag screws ⅜-in. diameter, 4 in. long and washers to fit.

Post and Rail Fences *(fig. 36)*

Farm boys climb fences in the course of doing their chores and also for fun. City boys climb fences for fun and to show their daring. Both boys and girls enjoy climbing fences, walking on them, and sitting on them, yet few parents think of providing them for exercise and recreation. Nevertheless, children living in cities and suburbs react to fences the same as other children—witness the popularity of the occasional board fence found around a school yard.

It may seem silly to a homeowner to build a section of fence merely for children to climb over, and the truth is that a section of fence standing in a yard where there seems to be no utilitarian need for it would cause a good many laughs. However, in most yards a use can be found. For example, a short section of fence can be built to separate the vegetable garden from the lawn. Another possibility is separation of the laundry drying area from the lawn, and still another is division of the children's play area from the adults'. Whatever the excuse, build the fence so that it can be climbed and walked on and it will return its cost as much used, low-maintenance play equipment.

The kind of fence shown in Fig. 36 A is very easy to make if you can obtain the small poles. Poles 4 to 8 in. in diameter are a handy size. Notice that poles are used for the posts as well as for the horizontal rails. The blocking that joins the upright pairs of posts can be waste lumber of any dimensions that make good cleats. The cleats are simply nailed to the posts with nails. Aluminum nails are preferred in order to avoid rust stains.

Although the sketch indicates that the fence is continuous at both ends, the purpose is to indicate how the overlapping poles are placed over one another. If a single section only is built, there will be, of course, no overlapping poles.

As with all wood placed in the ground, thought must be given to warding off decay and insect attack if you wish the fence to last more than two or three seasons. Unless you can obtain wood in post form which has a high degree of resistance to these destructive agents, it will be advisable to soak the portions of the posts that will be placed in the ground and about 6 in. more with a wood preservative (Introduction).

Usually no attempt is made to put fence posts below the frost line;

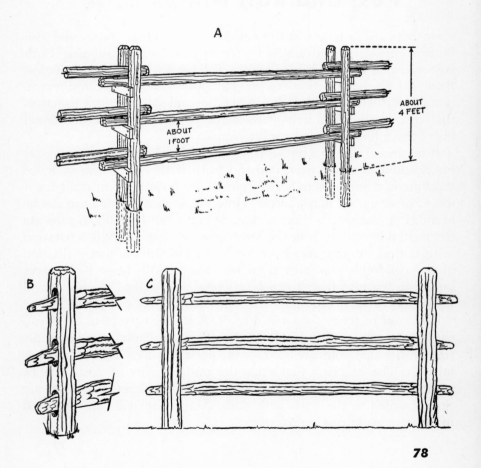

hence the only requirement for depth is enough of it to make the fence firm. Holes dug about 2 ft. deep should anchor the posts solidly enough if the soil is packed in carefully around them. There is nothing fixed about the distance between the pairs of upright posts. It should hardly be less than 6 or 7 ft. even if the chief purpose of the fence is to provide a place for climbing and sitting. On the other hand, if poles of the small diameters suggested are longer than 10 or 12 ft. between supports, they may be too limber for good climbing.

Recommended Materials

Lumber

For the horizontal poles and the vertical posts: Peeled logs of any wood that is known in the locality to give satisfactory service as fence posts.

Post and rail fences such as the one sketched in Fig. 36 B and C are essentially a variation of the kind just described, but from the construction standpoint the difference is considerable. Although a home-owner who is skilled with woodworking tools can make such a fence, this variety is usually purchased ready-made from the manufacturers and dealers in fences. The posts are one piece and come with the holes cut in them. At their ends the poles are hewed down to a smaller dimension to enable them to pass through the holes in the posts. When there is more than one length of fence, the ends of posts of adjacent sections are placed side by side in the holes.

Since both the posts and the rails are purchased ready for assembly, there is nothing to do but dig the holes. Usually even the wood preservation treatment is taken care of at the factory.

The holes should be dug to the necessary depth. The posts are stood in them and tipped so that their tops tilt away from one another. The ends of the bottom rail are then placed in the bottom holes in the two posts. Next, the middle rail is put in place, and finally the third one. The posts are then pushed up to vertical positions and the holes around them are filled with well tamped soil.

Recommended Materials

Lumber

Factory-made posts and rails. The rails should be selected for freedom from coarse knots and any other defects which would make them unsuitable for climbing.

Board Fences *(fig. 37)*

The fence illustrated in Fig. 37 A and B is from some standpoints the best kind for small children to climb because its surfaces are all flat and provide fairly good footing even when wet. In contrast, the round logs used in the other styles of fences can be rather slippery when wet.

As shown in the drawings, this fence is made entirely of 4 by 4's and 2 by 4's. If you desire a very attractive fence, the lumber should be dressed. Otherwise, rough lumber should serve. However, corners should be rounded and the top rail planed and sanded smooth.

Since 4 by 4's are rather small for fence posts, the holes for them should be dug about 2½ ft. deep and should not be made any larger in diameter than necessary. The sections should not be too long or the top rail will not be as stiff as is desirable. Spacing the upright posts so that 2 by 4's in 8-ft. lengths may be used is strongly recommended. Two 8-ft. sections joined as shown in Fig. 37 B make a very satisfactory play fence.

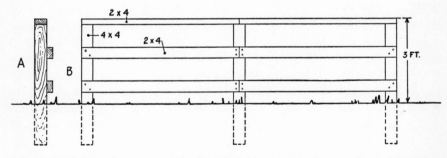

This fence is built as follows: The holes are dug for two adjacent posts and the posts are placed in them. The posts are connected with one of the horizontal members, preferably the top rail, then are made level in relation to each other and plumb. The soil is then packed around the posts. The two remaining horizontal pieces are then secured to the posts. Galvanized wood screws may be used for attaching

80

the 2 by 4's to the posts, but common nails go in much faster.

When the first section has been completed, the third post hole is dug and the second section of fence is erected in the same way.

Recommended Materials

Lumber

No. 2 pine or other locally available construction lumber. The bottoms of the posts should be treated with a wood preservative (Introduction).

Hardware

Zinc-plated lag screws ⅜-in. diameter, 4 in. long, or 16-penny spikes.

Playhouses *(figs. 38 to 43)*

Playhouses are often regarded as luxury toys, the sort of thing that rich people provide for their children, but that people of lesser means can do without as they do without butlers. This seems to me to be the wrong attitude. Girls who watch their mothers doing housework may get more fun out of a playhouse than the daughters of very wealthy families whose mothers do no housework. Girls from the kindergarten age almost up to the age of high school will enjoy a playhouse more than any other kind of toy except dolls, and, of course, dolls and a playhouse go together naturally.

A playhouse large enough actually to be played in is not inexpensive, nor easy to construct. Building it is a good deal like building a house in miniature. In fact, in some localities, one must get a building permit in order to erect a playhouse in one's yard. Nevertheless, playhouses are built all the time by amateurs, and some very good ones have been built by those who never built a full-sized house.

Just as houses for adults may range from shacks to mansions, there are no upper or lower limits to the construction of a playhouse. They may be extremely simple, or they can be as strongly built and as fully detailed as full-scale houses. Since playhouses are eventually outgrown and are not readily available, it is seldom advisable for a parent of modest means to make one that is very elaborate.

The fact that a playhouse is exposed to the weather, including in most localities heavy rain and high winds, makes it necessary to give it a fairly strong frame. The elements of a standard frame are shown in Fig. 38 A, and the most important parts are identified there by name. Fig. 38 B shows the relations among the ridge, rafters, and plate when the rafters do not project beyond the plate. Fig. 38 C shows their relations when the rafters project to form an overhang for the roof. The elements of a frame for a lean-to playhouse, that is, one built against the wall of another building, are shown in Fig. 39.

The standard framing lumber for the construction of such frames

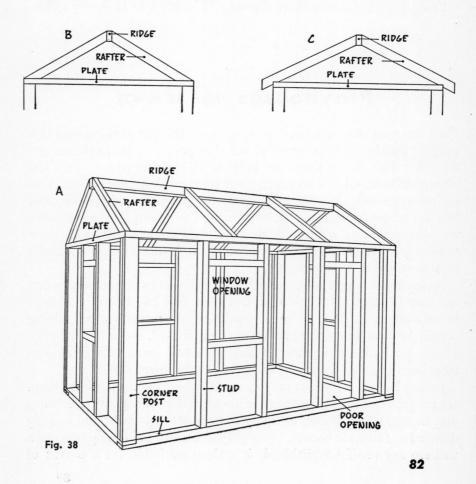

Fig. 38

is 2 in. by 4 in. in cross section and is usually referred to as 2 by 4's. In a playhouse 2 by 4's may be used for the sill, the studs, the plate, the rafters, and the ridge. The corner posts are made of two 2 by 4's spiked together for extra strength. The standard spacing for the studs in the frame of a full-sized house is 16 in. measured from the center line of one to the center line of the next. This spacing is all right for playhouses; a wider spacing, such as 24 in. center to center, may also be adopted.

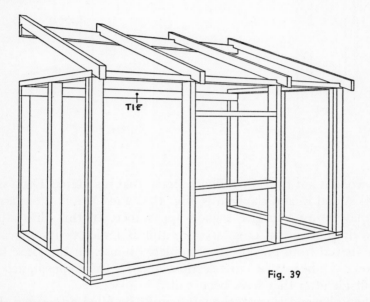

Fig. 39

The framework is covered on the outside with sheathing and siding or both. Usually for a playhouse a material is chosen that will serve as both sheathing and siding; that is to say, it will at the same time cover the framing and finish the exterior wall.

The appearance of a playhouse after its frame has been partly covered with exterior-type plywood is shown in Fig. 40. Here c and d represent two standard panels of plywood which have been cut to make the window and door openings. Exterior-type plywood is also an excellent material for finishing the roof, b, and closing the gable ends, a, of a playhouse. The plywood or any other siding material used is nailed to the structural elements of the frame. These nails are not indicated in the drawing.

83

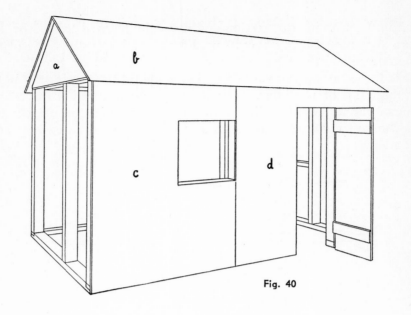

Fig. 40

Plywood is not the only siding material that is suitable. Drop siding, Fig. 41 A and B, and clapboards, Fig. 41 C and D, are other materials that may be used to give a good appearance. In this illustration A shows drop siding in cross section, and B indicates its appearance when viewed from outside the completed house. In the same figure, C shows clapboards in cross section, and D, their appearance from the outside after they have been nailed in place.

When plywood is used, the joints must be filled or covered. Joints between the plywood panels at the roof ridge may be made water-tight by covering them with an inverted V-shaped strip of a suitable metal such as zinc, copper, or galvanized steel. Joints between the panels on side walls may simply be filled with a caulking compound or they may be covered with a narrow strip of wood called a batten. Batten strips are available from all lumber dealers.

Joints in other types of roofing and siding are usually more numer-ous but are simpler to make because of some integral feature of the material. The views of drop siding and clapboards (Fig. 41) will give an idea of how the joint problem is solved in these materials. Joints in most roofing materials are made rain-tight by overlapping. Usually for such materials as shingle roofing, boards or strips are nailed crosswise of the rafters, then the roofing shingles or strips are nailed to them. Fig. 41 E shows a section through a shingle roof. It also shows how at a difficult joint such as the one between a building wall and the roof of a lean-to playhouse, a strip of metal called flashing is run under the shingles to turn water.

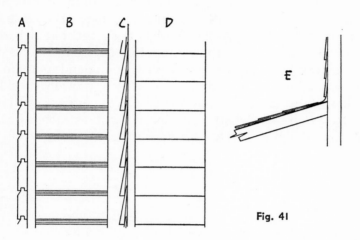

Fig. 41

Elaborate windows such as are installed in full-size houses are not to be recommended for playhouses because simpler types will serve. A kind that is simple to install in a window opening such as the one in Fig. 40 is shown in Fig. 42. This window opens outward and is hinged at one side. When closed, it presses against a narrow, inside frame which renders it reasonably wind- and water-tight. The sliding type of window is also a good one for playhouses. A variety of this is shown in Fig. 43. Installation is a little more difficult than a hinged window because a notch (Fig. 43 B) must be cut in a stud to permit the window to slide past. Wind will not blow off a sliding window, and such a window is never in a position where boys on the outside of the house can swing on it.

Playhouse exterior doors can be elaborate or simple. An example of the latter kind is shown in Fig. 40. As can be seen, this door is constructed of a section of plywood panel and two broad cleats. If a better door is desired, consider buying a closet door, either new or used, from a dealer in second-hand building supplies.

In Fig. 40 the door is shown extending all the way to the ground, and the sill has been cut so as not to obstruct the passage. In contrast, a sill that is continuous across the door opening is shown in Fig. 38 A. Which type is suitable depends upon how the floor of the playhouse is to be constructed.

Often playhouses are simply put down on the ground. This exposes the sill to moisture, and decay and termite attack may follow soon. On the other hand, it does not add a great deal to the cost of making a playhouse to provide it with a foundation that will hold it out of contact with the soil. A suitable foundation is a concrete slab about 6 in. thick and extending over the entire area occupied by the playhouse. Such a slab can be coated with an asphalt compound in a 4-in. band around its perimeter. This asphalt band will provide considerable protection against dampness and insects. On the interior of the house the concrete slab may be left plain, but it will be a more satisfactory floor if it is covered with standard asphalt tile.

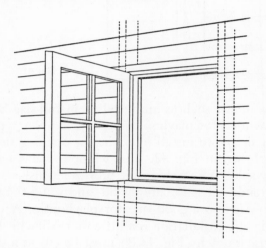

Fig. 42

Assuming that you elect to build a foundation and to use asphalt tile, the sill should be cut away from the door and the door extended down to the ground level as shown in Fig. 40. Another method of foundation construction is to build a foundation of concrete block all around the perimeter of the house. After the foundation has been built, the sill is placed on the block foundation, which stands up from the ground 8 in. or more. If this kind of foundation is used, or if the sill is placed directly on the earth, the sill should be continuous at the door opening because the floor in the playhouse will be above the level of the top of the sill.

86

A practical way of building such a floor is to lay tongued-and-grooved lumber of ¾-in. nominal thickness from sill to sill parallel to the shorter dimension of the house. This lumber should rest on the sills and be nailed to it. In order to keep its underside from becoming unduly damp, the ground under the house should be covered with overlapping layers of a heavy asphalt-impregnated roofing paper. Many kinds of floor covering from inexpensive asphalt tile to genuine wall-to-wall broadloom carpeting may be installed on top of the tongued-and-grooved flooring. If the floor is above the sill, a shorter door and a shallow stone step on the outside of the house will be needed to make the front entrance look right.

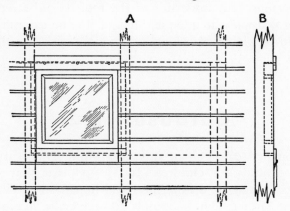

Fig. 43

When the playhouse has a foundation, a frame, a roof, a floor, windows and doors, and its exterior walls are covered, it is usually ready for occupancy. The matter of finishing the interior remains, and sometimes this is done down to the last detail. However, many a playhouse has been used with great pleasure by a large family of girls and boys without any interior finishing. After all, the pictures, furniture, window curtains, and other things soon hide the rough walls or render them unobtrusive to the playhouse's happy occupants.

There is no space in this book for a description of the many other building techniques that are of interest in playhouse construction—for instance, how to paint, how to hang doors, how to lay flooring, etc. I can only assume that if you are building a playhouse you live in a house. If you do, you will be able to learn by studying it most of these things that you need to know for application in the playhouse. For example, you can look at a door and see how the hinges are placed.

87

For the techniques of such operations as the laying of asphalt tile, your local librarian will undoubtedly be able to refer you to books in which such things are fully described in simple language.

Good dimensions for a playhouse depend primarily on how many children will use it. A floor area 8 ft. by 10 ft. is plenty of space for one or two little girls, whereas a family of three or four girls will need 10 ft. by 12 ft. or even 12 ft. by 14 ft. If there is some question about the needed area why not let the girls set up their play housekeeping temporarily in one of the bedrooms of your house and find out how large these areas are? There should be no real partitions, only pretend ones, in a playhouse, so as to take full advantage of the floor area. Furthermore, the underside of the roof should serve as the ceiling. Six feet is usually an adequate height for the exterior door. Windows should be placed at a height where the girls can operate them easily.

Carousel *(fig. 44)*

A child-propelled carousel, or merry-go-round, is a feature of most public playgrounds for children. It is a popular play device with most of the elementary school group, although some children suffer from giddiness on it. The carousels commercially manufactured for public playgrounds are rather expensive affairs because the central shaft and bearing on which the platform revolves must be very strong. In addition, the apparatus requires a rather sturdy foundation. The average homeowner would not be inclined either to spend the necessary money for a device of this kind or to give it room in his yard.

The carousel sketched in Fig. 44 is by contrast a tiny device designed for simultaneous use by three or four children at most. It cannot be whirled with the speed of the commercial ones (which many parents will consider to be in its favor), and it will not continue to rotate so long after the pushing ceases. In spite of these disadvantages, it is a thrilling toy, especially for children from about 4 years to about 10. It has the further advantage of being neither costly nor difficult to build.

A sketch of the complete carousel is shown at Fig. 44 A. As can be seen here, the platform or part on which the children stand is made of six wedge-shaped sections of plywood. Each of these sections is a triangle having three equal sides. Three of them may be cut from a standard 4-ft. by 8-ft. plywood panel as shown in Fig. 44 E. The triangular sections of plywood are supported by a three-membered frame shown in Fig. 44 B as it would appear if you looked straight down on it with the platform out of the way. Wheels are attached to the ends of the three members of the frame, and the railing is attached to the top of the platform. The relations of these essential parts, the wheels, the frame, the platform and the railing, can be seen in Fig. 44 C.

The central bearing which can be seen in C and D serves primarily to keep the merry-go-round from wandering off. It bears none of the weight and its construction allows the carousel to be lifted up when necessary to clear leaves and rubbish from underneath.

The concrete base on which the merry-go-round runs is an important part of it and is usually constructed first. It should be made of rather dense concrete and should be at least 6 in. thick; and under the center bearing it should be made deeper so as to provide a thickness of not less than 4 in. under the center post. Some wire reinforcing placed 2 or 3 in. beneath the top surface will help to prevent cracks.

The center post may be a steel pipe of 2½-in. or 3-in. nominal diameter or a steel rod of 2½-in. actual diameter. The post should not be permanently fixed in the cement because of the hazard it would present when the merry-go-round is picked up and stored indoors for the winter. To prevent its sticking in the concrete it should be greased with automobile engine oil or cup grease before the concrete is poured.

A simple way to get this pipe into position and to hold it there while the concrete is being placed is to select a length of stiff plank 2 or 3 ft. longer than the diameter of the excavation and bore a hole through it in which the pipe will fit snugly. The pipe is then placed in this hole with the end projecting. The projecting end should be measured to make certain that an adequate length will be in the concrete. After the pipe has been fixed in the hole in the plank, its lower end should be closed by wadding it tightly with a rag. Finally, the outside of the pipe and the bottom of the plank are greased. Before placing of the concrete begins, the plank is placed across the excavation so that the pipe is held in the desired position. The ends of the plank are then firmly staked down.

Not more than an hour after the concrete is placed, the top surface should be worked to a smooth finish with a steel trowel. Smoothness is particularly important in the portion of the concrete base where the wheels will run. If the plank holding the center post is in the way of the trowel, it may be wedged up near its ends with shingles or thin boards enough to permit the trowel to be slipped under it.

After troweling, the surface of the concrete should be covered with some old rags or straw, or other light materials that will hold moisture, and sprinkled with a fine mist from the garden hose. Unless this is done the top surface will not be hard enough and will powder away under use. After 24 hours the plank and the center post may be lifted clear and the hole will remain open.

Construction of the merry-go-round itself usually begins with the sawing out of six triangular pieces. The frame is built next. The three members of it, 6 in. or 8 in. wide, may be cut from plywood or from board lumber. It simplifies construction to cut them all from the same thickness of plywood or lumber. The two lower members are then built up with additional strips of lumber to the level of the first strip. The lumber strips that serve to build up these members can be seen in Fig. 44 D. Finally, the three members of the underframe are joined by two long bolts. The position of these bolts can be seen in Fig. 44 B and D.

Next, the triangular sections of the platform are fastened to the three members of the underframe. Either nails or wood screws may be used, but the latter are to be preferred. If screws are used, they should be placed about ½ in. from the edges of the panels and must be long enough to penetrate the wood underneath at least ½ inch. This means screws of varying lengths depending upon whether the screw enters directly over solid wood or must first pass through one of the empty spaces between the built-up edges of the frame members. Even when screws are used, it is a good idea to use carriage bolts at the outer edges of the panels.

Once the platform and framing members are fastened together, turn the platform top side down and attach the center bearing and the wheels. Details of the center bearing may be seen in Fig. 44 D. Actually, it consists only of a steel cup of the right internal diameter to slip over the center post. If the center post is of unthreaded pipe, the bearing can be made of a standard pipe cap. Ream out part or all

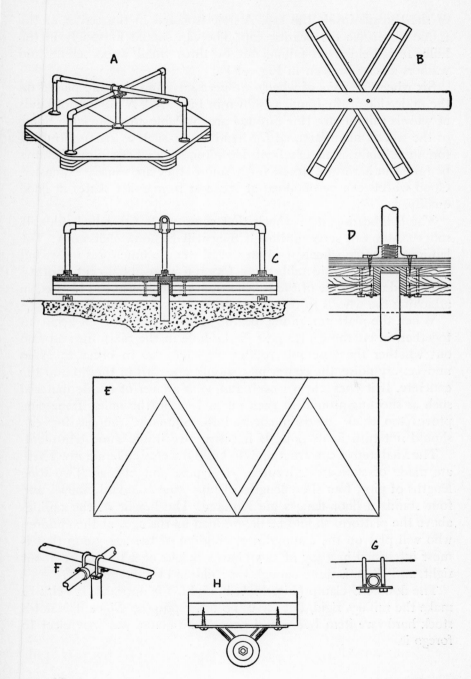

91

of the threads inside the cap. A hole is bored in the center of the frame to receive the bearing cap. The cap should fit snugly in the hole. It is held from falling out by three small wood screws and washers as can be seen in Fig. 44 D.

Six wheels or pairs of wheels are necessary, and they are placed on the underside of the frame as shown in Fig. 44 C. A number of kinds of wheels suitable for this carousel are available commercially. Some of the wheels manufactured for hand trucks such as are used in factories and libraries are excellent. However, such wheels cannot always be found in hardware stores; furthermore, they are usually expensive. Good wheels can be obtained at less cost from roller skates of good quality.

The ball-bearing steel wheels that come on the so-called sidewalk roller skates will serve, although they will be somewhat noisy. The laminated maple wheels used on rink skates are much less noisy, but such skates cost considerably more. Often it is possible to cut or otherwise divide the frame of the roller skate so that it also can be used in attaching the wheels to the merry-go-round frame (Fig. 44 H).

When the platform, frame, bearing, and wheels have all been put together, insert the center post in the hole in the platform and find out whether the ensemble rotates satisfactorily. In order to avoid unnecessary noise, the center post should not turn in the hole in the concrete. If it does, clean it well and wrap a layer of textile material such as sheeting around it, then put it back in the hole. If sheeting proves too thick, try thin cheesecloth. Similarly, the bearing cap should not turn in its hole. If it turns, give it the same treatment.

The final step in construction is to build the crossed handrails. These are made of standard galvanized steel pipe and fittings. Two long lengths of pipe, four short lengths of pipe, four standard elbows, and four standard floor flanges are required. The height of the railings above the platform should be determined by the ages of the children who will play on the carousel. For children of the age group that is most interested in a toy of this kind, a height of 2 ft. will be about right, and 18 in. is quite enough for children of pre-school age.

The double-U clamp (Fig. 44 A, F, and G) is optional. It helps to make the railings rigid, but serves no other purpose. Since it is not a stock hardware item but would have to be made, you may elect to forego it.

Recommended Materials

Concrete

For the concrete base: A 1:2:3 mix (Introduction) containing no gravel larger than 1 in. in diameter.

Lumber

For the platform: Exterior-type plywood of ¾-in. or 1-in. thickness.

For the underframe: Exterior-type plywood plus a knot-free board lumber for building up; or No. 1 pine boards, or an equivalent lumber of adequate strength.

Hardware

For the wheels: High-quality, ball-bearing steel roller-skate wheels; or ball-bearing, high-quality laminated maple roller-skate wheels; or ball-bearing rubber-tired hand-truck wheels.

For the center post: Galvanized steel pipe or plain steel rod of the sizes mentioned above.

For the railings: Galvanized steel pipe of 1-in. nominal diameter. Standard elbows and floor flanges to fit.

For attaching the floor flanges: No. 10 1¼-in. galvanized steel screws.

For attaching the wheels: No. 10 1½-in. galvanized steel screws with round heads.

For fastening the platform and the frame: Galvanized carriage bolts and galvanized wood screws of appropriate length.

Tricycle Runs *(figs. 45 to 46)*

The benefits of the motor age are many, but they are not all apparent to a small child with a tricycle who has been instructed to remain off the street. Or if the child happens to live on a road or street where there is no sidewalk, it will not be clear to him where he may ride his first wheeled toy. In our larger cities the authorities who plan and maintain public parks have come to the rescue of horse riders who found themselves in the same predicament from the same cause.

Probably in a few parks some stretches of sidewalk have been set aside for the benefit of the tricycle group, but certainly such provisions are uncommon. In many homes it is up to the parent to provide a place for safe enjoyment of a tricycle, and in a good many homes the parents fail to do this.

The yard plans that were so much in vogue two or three decades ago and earlier did not lend themselves to the making of tricycle runs. There was much emphasis on a spacious front lawn, and much of the back yard was devoted to the hanging out of laundry. The garage (or stable) was placed at the rear of the lot at the end of a long and often unpaved driveway. Fortunately things have changed. Now people develop their yards for outdoor living. Patios, paved driveways, and paved walks are common features. Often, though, there is a missing link if you look at the yard from the viewpoint of a 3-year-old on his first 3-wheeled vehicle.

What a tricycler needs is a walk on which he can travel around and around. A narrow walk where he has to pedal back and forth is not much fun. How a route of the required kind can be provided in typical yards is shown in Figs. 45 and 46. In Fig. 45 A is a typical "remodeled" yard. The garage is at the rear of the lot and the house

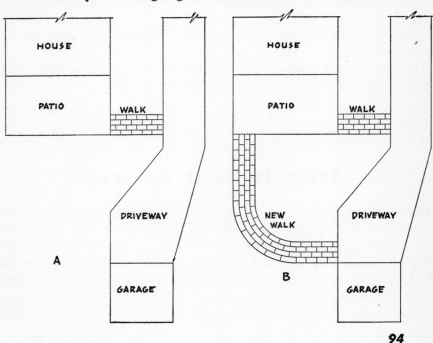

is at the front, but a new patio has been constructed and a walk connects the driveway with the patio. Now, if the driveway is hard-surfaced, making a good tricycle run requires only the construction of the new walk shown in Fig. 45 B. Here is a circuit that a young rider will enjoy. Not only is it fairly long and continuous, but it contains points of interest such as the garage, the patio, and the house.

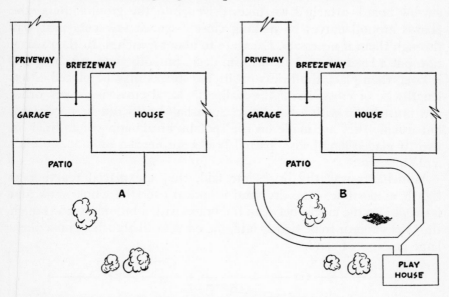

In Fig. 46 a more modern yard layout is shown. Obviously not much can be done at the front to provide a safe tricycle track. A plain circular or oval walk at the rear of the house would not be much fun because of its monotony. In addition, it would look a little nonsensical in the landscape. However, provide a focal point of interest, such as a playhouse at the rear of the lot, and the problem is solved.

Inasmuch as small tricycles and very young riders require rather smooth pavements for traveling, a walk whose main purpose is the encouragement of riding at home should be well built. Concrete can be used to produce smooth walks, but unfortunately it is unattractive. Flagstones are attractive and popular, but they tend to be bumpy, especially if turf is allowed to grow between the stones. Brick is a little rough, but if the bricks are carefully laid young riders will not complain.

If you do not mind a little annual maintenance, a good brick walk can be constructed easily. Assuming that the yard has good drainage so that the soil is not soggy most of the time, a brick walk can be built without a foundation. Frost may heave some of the brick during the winter, but they can be put back in place in the spring.

To build a brick walk in well drained soil, proceed as follows: First stake out the route with stakes and string or, better still, with narrow boards attached to stakes driven into the ground. Bend the boards around curves by making closely spaced saw cuts part way through them if necessary. Excavate to about 6 inches. In the excavation put a layer of sand about 3 in. deep. Smooth the sand so that it is level, then place the bricks on it. The bricks may be placed either lengthwise or crosswise of the walk. If placed crosswise, every other row must begin with a half-brick. Such half-bricks can be purchased, but usually they are made on the spot by breaking a whole brick in two. If placed lengthwise, partial bricks are needed only at the ends and on curves.

Whichever way the bricks are laid, they are placed together as tightly as possible. Fine dry sand is spread over the whole walk and is swept into the cracks between the bricks with a broom. Even though the bricks appear to be tightly laid, the cracks will absorb an amazingly large amount of sand.

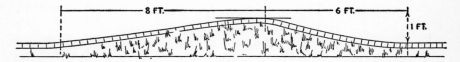

A hump in a walk in a yard will seem perfectly useless to adults, but it will be fun for young tricyclers. First, it will help the rank beginners to learn, for they can coast down the slope until they learn to propel with the pedals. After the rider has become sophisticated, he will enjoy the thrill of cresting the hill, then swooping down. How such a hump might be proportioned is shown in Fig. 47. (In order to make the drawing clear, the bricks have been shown on top of the soil, although in an actual walk they would be level with its surface.)

Flowing Brook
with Waterfall *(fig. 48)*

One of the best things that can happen to a family of normal children is to have Nature and Fortune place their home where they have access to a flowing brook. Unfortunately, Nature and Fortune are kind in this way to relatively few children. Only children in the country inevitably find their way to streams for play. It seems a novel idea to many people who live on city lots to learn that it is possible to make an artificial brook. I know of no way of making one on an absolutely level plot, but if your land has a slope—and it need not be a very steep one—an artificial brook is a practical though somewhat expensive idea.

Such a brook depends upon an electric pump to make it function. The pump gets its water from a tank buried under ground, and the water simply makes one round trip after another. Because the water slowly evaporates or otherwise disappears, it must be added to the system from time to time.

The elements of an artificial brook are sketched (not too realistically) in Fig. 48. At A is shown a plan view, in other words, a diagram of the installation as it would appear from the air. The heavy, wavy lines outline the brook's course. The relative positions of the filter, supply pipe, drain, and pump house are shown; possible spots for a small waterfall and a tiny pool are also shown. The sketch marked *B* is a section drawing taken vertically through the same system. This drawing shows, again, the relative positions of the pump house, the buried tank, and the filter, and also indicates how the supply pipe runs underground. The concrete sections that form the bed of the brook and prevent loss of the water can be seen in section in this drawing.

Obviously an artificial brook must be designed for a particular site. Unless it is carefully planned, it will be neither attractive nor interesting. However, some thought and ingenuity can make it a valuable landscape feature as well as a plaything of unbelievable interest.

All of the hydraulic and mechanical parts can be bought readily. They are available as new ones; in addition, most of them can be purchased second-hand at considerably reduced prices. The pump may be of several types; for example, a piston pump such as is often found in farm water-supply systems is quite suitable. On the other hand, the centrifugal pump is an inexpensive and trouble-free type, and it should work very well except in installations where the water must be lifted to a height greater than 20 feet. Horizontal distance does not count, only the vertical distance from the pump to the highest point reached by the water in the system. Preferably the pump installation and the electric wiring should be designed and installed by experts.

The tank can be almost any closed steel tank such as an old gasoline or oil tank. If one can be found with only a leak or two, these can probably be repaired. However, do not install a tank that seems badly corroded. A tank that has been used for some such substance as fuel oil should be thoroughly cleaned before being put to use in this system to avoid staining of the concrete. Oily substances can usually be cleaned out with plenty of water and household detergent.

Plastic piping of the kind used for underground piping in farm water systems and widely sold by hardware stores and general mail-order houses is the best for connecting the pump tank and filter. The filter is simply a strong wooden box filled with alternate layers of sand and gravel. There is an opening in the bottom of the box for the discharge of the water. A fine screen is placed over this opening; a layer of coarse gravel about 3 in. thick goes on the bottom of the box; then comes a layer of medium-fine sand about 2 in. thick, then another layer of coarse gravel, and finally a layer of fine sand.

The bed of the stream is made of concrete, and because of the length of the bed the concrete must be cast in sections. Except that the sections are purposely made irregular, the bed is made by the same technique as for a concrete sidewalk. After the concrete has become firm, the joints between the sections are filled with a cold-setting asphalt compound. This technique produces flexible, water-tight joints. Finally, the banks of the stream are turfed and planted so as to give it a natural look.

In order to make the water flow, the pump must operate. However, water will stand in the pools when the pump is not operating; therefore, even at such times the stream will be interesting to dabble in. If the stream bed has been planned right, it will not take an unduly large flow of water to make interesting waterfalls and swift currents between the pools. A pump that will cause a flow of 15 to 20 gallons a minute should be large enough. In an arid climate evaporation will be rather rapid, but even in such regions a tankful of water will last many days. In humid regions rain often keeps the tank full.

98

Maintenance of the system, aside from keeping the pump in working order, consists in removing trash. Coarse trash such as leaves will be caught on the drain at the lower end and can be picked off. Finer materials will collect on the top of the sand in the filter. They can be scraped off together with a little sand, after which a small quantity of fresh sand is added.

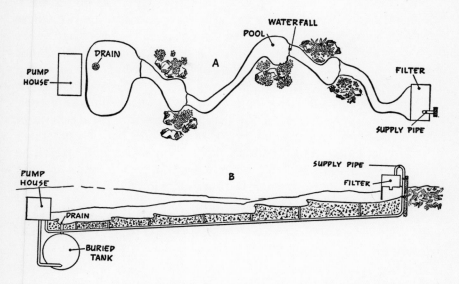

In cold regions the system must be designed for draining before winter comes. This feature also should be planned by an expert in the installation of pumps. In the system sketched in Fig. 48, most of the water can be pumped out simply by attaching a hose to the pipe at the upper end and diverting the water so that it does not enter the filter. Your pump will almost certainly have a drain plug that can be opened to take the last remnants of water out of it. A few inches of water remaining in the tank will not burst it because there will be plenty of room for expansion of the ice. To prevent the tank from being filled by rain or melting snow, the drain should be carefully plugged or capped over.